Reveries of the Wild Woman

AGM COLLECTION

AVANT-GARDE & MODERNISM

Reveries of the Wild Woman

Primal Scenes

HÉLÈNE CIXOUS

Translated from the French by Beverley Bie Brahic

Northwestern

University Press

Evanston

Illinois

Northwestern University Press
www.nupress.northwestern.edu

Printed in the United States of America

10 9 8 7 6 5 4 3 2 1

ISBN 0-8101-2363-0

Library of Congress Cataloging-in-Publication data are available
from the Library of Congress.

⊚ The paper used in this publication meets the minimum
requirements of the American National Standard for Information
Sciences—Permanence of Paper for Printed Library Materials,
ANSI Z39.48-1992.

Les rêveries de la femme sauvage: Scènes primitives *publié avec le
concours du Ministère français chargé de la culture/Centre national du
livre.* [Reveries of the Wild Woman: Primal Scenes is published with
support from the French Ministry of Culture/National Book Center.]

Reveries of the Wild Woman

"The whole time I was living in Algeria I would dream of one day arriving in Algeria, I would have done anything to get there, I had written, I never made it to Algeria, it is right now that I must explain what I mean by this, how I longed for the door to open, now not later, I had scribbled, in the fever of the July night, for it is now, and probably for dozens or hundreds of reasons that a door has cracked opened in the Oblivion Wing of my memory, and now for the first time I may be able to return to Algeria, therefore I must . . ."

I had written that in the middle of a July night and as sometimes happens when a book shows up, always in the middle of the night, awaited of course, yearned for with extreme patience, capable of all conceivable and inconceivable acts of trust and humility, I had written these lines, under the influence of the longed-for but unimaginable upwelling of the book which therefore did wish to respond to my infinitely timid supplications and therefore as usual in such cases of nocturnal manifestation, I had written without turning on the light so as not to risk scaring the Comer off, quick, without a sound, I grab the pad of paper that never leaves my bedside and the thick-tipped pen for scribbling big across the page, and I had noted the first lines that the Comer dictated to me, hastily covering a good-sized page with the priceless sentences, yeast of the book, gift of gods whose names I don't even know. Once the absolute viaticum had been received I ventured to switch on the light, and as though I held the Host to disperse the Comer's flesh and blood through my body in my mouth, in my soul's mouth and my hand's, and on my night tongue, as I let it dissolve, in the trace of that initial seeding, I had scrawled four big, single-spaced pages, fragrant with ink earth galloping sweat panting nostrils, but pages vivid fleshed-out, powerful dense, full of a stirring generosity, I was jubilant, I'll

3

thank the donors tomorrow morning, I thought, four immense pages with every sign of being viable, which for me means I have only to forge ahead, once I've been given the beginning, I have only to press on, you have to work with all your might, naturally, but the essential is there, the rest is possible and requires only an extraordinary mustering of energy.

So I was up at dawn, ready to set to work, radiant. Fulfilled: all night long, through an abundant flow of dreams and the chaos of civilizations Algeria had sent me a sea of traces, visions, relaying packages across thousands of obstacles, bringing totally forgotten people to life, good as new, you imagine there's nothing left in the rubble, but have a peek over the railing here, what do you see?! Mohamed! I saw: Mohamed! who must have died ages ago, and not only did I see him but I could smell him and I thought I am not so poor and deserted as I believe. Mohamed in person ensconced in the stairwell on the Philippe Street. I had scrawled a few words on the paper to give an idea of Mohamed: tin pans burlap bags and who knows what else.

And now I couldn't set hand on them. Of the five pages I had written with unrestrained joy, which I am not making up, for I saw them written down, I could find only half a sheet, the first one, upon which I had written, without even switching on the light, the lines "*The whole time I was living in Algeria,* etc." up to "*therefore I must*" the rest had disappeared, which was not possible.

I started searching, there are lots of papers around, hundreds, a thousand maybe, and I didn't find them. I began searching again, more and more methodically and more and more irritably, I was boiling and pulled off a sweater, I riffled through files where only madness could have induced me to put those sheets, I searched the same files again immediately afterward, pretty soon I couldn't stop searching and not finding them, thinking deliriously there was no way I could stop looking for them without having found them it was getting to be a matter of life and death, but I could do nothing except sift, turn over, leaf through hundreds of pages, nothing on earth could have put a halt to my frenzy, two hours had passed already, two hours which means the hours most precious to me, the ones I'd set aside for rewriting in the light of day the famous pages night had granted me, hours which had veered from hope to the most raging despair, beyond a doubt I was digging my grave, the idea of suicide began to permeate the pit of paper, and even as I told myself to desist I stepped up the pace of the deadly digging, it never entered my mind to try and recall those pages, the idea of reconstituting them was unacceptable, I wanted those ones, the very ones that had been given me and which by an utterly inexplicable sleight of hand had vanished into thin air.

Of course, it stood to reason they existed somewhere. But I stood facing a wall that I groped at sobbing without finding the door. In addition, around eleven a.m. there was an inexplicable heavenly phenomenon: the sky grew totally black, and night fell. This is a fact. This incredible night rumbling with thunder, but dry, lasted an hour. In the midst of this night which held day off until noon, all lamps ablaze, I searched and searched. I could do nothing else. I took note in passing of the concordance of the signs. But nothing could release me from my moral obligation, and nobody could have broken the atrocious spell that bound me. I pondered this in a corner of my mind: only a death my mother's maybe could have snapped the chains, yes maybe only that. Some kind of suffering able to vie with the suffering that held me clamped in irons. All that in the gloom and dark. I couldn't renounce *It*. One is going to die and there is no death. There is nothing worse I was thinking the way a candle flickers toward extinction my mind flickered there is nothing worse, but almost. To lose but incompletely to lose almost and to be relegated to the suffocating verge of death without being able to do a thing about it, and no other port or portal than die or dead. It's a horror film, just a movie we say perhaps but the horror is heartstopping.

Okay, I tell myself slowly between two cardiac spasms (and during this time, my mother who could see me fading away in anguish was searching everywhere, in the kitchen, in her buffet) at the end of the lost morning, devoted to madness, now this is exactly what used to happen with Algeria, when I was living there: I had it, I'd got a grip on it—I didn't have it any longer, I'd never had it, I'd never held it in my arms. Precisely: I'd go after it, and it wasn't too far off, I used to live in Algeria, in Oran to begin with then in Algiers, I was living *in* the city of Oran and I used to search for it after that I was living *in* the city of Algiers and I'd be looking for the entryway and it kept eluding me, on its own earth, beneath my feet I could never touch it, I wanted the door to open, now I have to find a way to tell about the expedition I threw myself into heart and soul looking for Algeria, how I spent the first part of my Oran life looking for the four pages, feverishly and relentlessly how I finally gave up, thinking I'd be able to when I got to Algiers in the second half of my day, how in the Clos-Salembier I had the glimmer of an illusion, corresponding to my mother's entry into my study half an hour ago, her face alight in hopes of resuscitating me, holding out a pad of paper! oh! I know it! from afar! my writing! and for a moment I believed I was saved but this pad no it's my dreambook which I've already leafed through ten times, it's not that it's not that, just as in the garden of the Clos-Salembier I would nestle against Aïcha the minute she lowered her veil in the little courtyard at the end of the section of the drive-way that runs along the right side of the house, at the kitchen door, with as witnesses the hens opposite and to the right locked in his cage the char-acter of Fips the dog, in imitation of whom my brother and I weren't yet aware we were alive—there, in this little cement plot called the yard, I snuggled up to Aïcha's body and laughing she let me hug her country for a fraction of a second and that was all, except for the hundreds of doors of the Clos-Salembier which, from beyond the garden grill, slid lowered eyes in our direction.

As a matter of fact the following pages had been about my mother and what she called her suicide that is the way she had occasioned her own loss in other words the Clinic, her work of art, her creation and her extraordi-nary mill for turning babies out into the light of Algerian day, an immense loss without equivalent, for unlike me she would never have left Algeria otherwise (other than by the misfortune called *involuntary suicide*). "*The whole time I was living in Algeria*" as I told myself with broad luminous strokes in those pages I couldn't yet bring myself to believe were gone, I had desired it and not just vaguely, distractedly, but urgently, with the dogged-ness of the head-over-heels-in-love, I could spend days and months posted in the streets, demanding a miracle, an arrival, an apparition, convinced I would obtain what I never did get by the sheer power of thought.

And to think that one day I about-faced and broke with this attachment. To think it is I who left, and my mother the German who stayed behind.

But in the end the one who didn't leave and who had never longed for nor broken with nor sought the one who always found her way without the least difficulty in the hairpin turns of the cities and shantytowns and who had never feared nor desired nor awaited nor gnashed her teeth and who with great regularity had kept the Clinic going turning out year after year several hundreds of newborns the one who unlike me was in the center and in the middle and in the interior, she's the one who once and precipitately was dismissed and given twenty-four hours to be out of the house. She who had never so much as dismissed a cleaning lady or midwife. She was fur-thermore so firmly implanted in the great uterus that only a violent abortive maneuver could have dislodged her. While I on the other hand had never ceased to hang by a thread to what was most uncertain right up to the day when exhausted by the work of joining that I myself performed I chose to call it quits.

It was this same anguish that was driving me crazy, the anguish of not finding the thing itself, whose author and creature I am, which I had in my hand, which is under my roof, among me, and which starts to take over, to invade me, invest my lungs, my ears, my head, saturating me with its absence, its withdrawal, which turns my whole body into a searing pain. But perhaps, I thought suddenly, this incomprehensible accident is not merely the sudden yawning of an abyss smack in the middle of my study on whose lip I crawl, perhaps it's not a hole in the universe or in my skull. Perhaps, I started to tell myself, during the thick night of noon which could hardly have been more realistic and nonetheless never-before-seen, it is not a weird and inauspicious occurrence. But quite the contrary. It is incredibly like that sort of *Algerian disorder* I used to get in Algeria or that Algeria got to me, that feeling of being possessed by a feeling of dispossession and the response I produced to this, that struggle to vanquish the unfindable that can lead to self-destruction, just like old times, here, in my study, after so many years. Prey to the unmournable my soul gnaws at me till it draws blood.

Then with an excruciating effort I broke with myself I severed myself I don't know how, it's as if I took hold of myself, and I dragged myself away from this scene of being sucked up. Next, still not knowing how, I made myself in two. And I put my own madness into my own work. By some kind of magic, I faced myself in the other direction. I had lost a treasure I couldn't replace. And this irreparable loss was going to take the place of the pages whose demise I could not yet admit, even if, as time went by, I was getting closer to giving up the search that is to giving up a limb of my soul.

—You didn't know Algeria, says my brother, he too given twenty-four hours to leave the known country, this was his sentence and its conclusion. This is how he attacks the subject. As usual we were sitting in the armchairs in which we take our places every time the scene in which we are the first couple gets underway again unbeknown to us. Naturally I don't see this scene when I am in it I am in the armchair it's only now stepping off to the side of the page that I see us and recognize the need for the chairs as guardrails. The room however calm it may appear is in fact buffeted by great gusts of violence, it looks as though we are talking to one another, but no idle chatter, in truth without appearing to leave our chairs it is titanic what we lift and overturn, a coastal country edged by a sea that we do not cease to heave up, bore into, traverse in all directions, the whole of the cemetery with its tombs whose stones monuments poor boxes we shake, putting our sorrows and anger together, like the crumbs of a filthy carnivorous banquet, the Cities, City of Oran and City of Algiers, beneath our bare feet—each time I catch sight of my brother's feet, his big toes curled over the steps, his way of gripping the world with his toes, I see my own feet of old, it is by our feet you see the relationship, the same feet, and they are my father's feet, the same way, my brother—my father, of taking Algeria by the soil—my brother never having stopped holding on and being held, I on the other hand having one day relaxed my grip and let go—and our bare feet feel the flexing of the seismic muscles of this ever-quaking earth. My brother's move. Always he who starts. The chess game is a fiction. A frail shadow of our give-and-take, a remains of the battle our father taught us. But I've noticed that each time we take our seats in the armchairs or almost, my brother leans forward, and each time I think he's going to play the knight. And me, the minute I can open up lines for the bishop I send him out. And both of us obviously protect the Queen. But in fact we have never set the chessboard up between us since our Clos-Salembier days.

None of what has gone back and forth between the armchairs over the decades has ever been insignificant. At the very least it is a plowing up with bones exhumed and the wreckage of moves, and it is often a war in which we are the original sworn brothers, shoulder to shoulder against the successive masks of the world enemy, joined in the battle against the world by the fire of an internal struggle which flares up again, which we rekindle when we meet by the friction of our equally sharp temperaments.

The minute we sit down in the chairs, my brother launches his attack. Always him who starts, I thought, head on, while when it's my turn to speak, I come from behind, over a shoulder or under a knee, but my brother is frontal. To be more precise: we head for the armchairs each time the demon of brotherhood nudges us in that direction. For the armchairs are the seat of brotherhood. In the armchairs I am next to my brother at his side and by his side on the one hand as the sister of a brother and on the other hand as an extra brother. Because if at home we rub one another till we flare up, facing the world we were always a single camp multiplied.

—You didn't know Algeria, he says, to conclude my opening remarks, after I read him the sentences salvaged from the disaster saying how I would have done anything to arrive in Algeria in the days I used to live there with my brother, at which point my brother bats it back with a flick of his wrist, an old trick, left over from our ping-pong games in the garden of the Clos-Salembier where we slashed mercilessly at the balls—the balls being needless to say condensed sentences.

"*Because when after waiting for five aching years which at our young age was as good as twenty we saw it appear at last that which had been lookedfor-beggedforhopedfor praised to high heaven its imaginary wheels stroked by our overexcited palms at each sacred occasion when it was logically if not reasonably permitted to imagine it coming*" I had jotted these lines on my pad, when my brother took the words out of my mouth as if he feared or foresaw rightly or wrongly that I might pinch the Bike story.

—Because when at last after so many years of fruitless waiting, painful and inexplicable except by something twisted, maybe even deranged in Mother's way of thinking who had no idea of the torture she inflicted on us, says my bother, by making us wait for this Bike which for us was not just any old bicycle and certainly not the two-wheeler Mother called it, but the simplest and most urgent means of escaping being shut up within walking range, a tool to conquer the country, and nonviolently what's more, which for us was bliss itself, this Bike then, whose name—*Le Vélo*—rang with everything we worshipped consciously or not, with Velocity and *lo* as in *l'eau* for water as in *le lot* for lots, and the *V* of Victory, the get-up-and-go and a great deal more, this Bike which would set us free, give us space height and therefore Algeria and all its inaccessible towns, when at last—my brother was off again, reliving and me too the years spent hanging on the promise of the Bike and me on the word *Bike* as well which is the beautifulest plain word in the world—when *finally we* got the Bike—yes *we* since this Bike which was supposed to be mine, *my* Bike, but which as a result of Mother's unforgivably foolish act—the act unforgivable, not being a man's Bike—and I could see my brother rigid with a fury at once ancient from forever and forever present new young, who not being able to bring himself even now to say "a girl's bike" preferred the euphemism "a bike which was not a man's"—could be used by you too, but then when we got the Bike, you never used it, at last you had the means to know Algeria beginning with the outskirts of the Clos-Salembier and beyond Birmandreis beyond Hydra beyond El Biar and beyond and at the moment when what had always been barred and refused was at last granted to us, and may I say to you above all, you never used it, but knowing I wouldn't fight you for it or keep you from using it I conclude that if you didn't get to know Algeria it's because you didn't give a hoot. You refused the Bike and therefore Algeria, thus spoke my brother and certainly the argument is valid. And that's why, sitting squarely in the little chair on the balcony he slams his big voice down on me.

—As for me, he shouts,

—since I didn't use the Bike, it's true, this is a fact, the Bike that was not a man's became my brother's, by a twist of fate and my mother's intention, which was to give my brother a unisex Bike. But who could have foreseen the immense and truly dramatic consequences of my mother's plan, in her eyes a perfectly normal plan justified by any number of economic factors and whose mental moral affective repercussions even today make themselves felt throughout the family and this we must hush up, in all the events, births marriages illnesses and deaths which happen to us, and in the choice of careers, partners, decisions, engagements, breakups, as well as in conversations around the family table. Everything that happened to us in the Clos-Salembier came in feminine and masculine and vice versa and we both needed and failed one another, I felt our couple tended to the masculine, but my brother claims the female side was uppermost, and all that came from the incessant nebulous Algerian sexual turbulence.

—As for me, shouts my brother, from that day I went off every day, from dawn to dusk exploring the country, and this despite the rage and shame which never left me, despite the unmerited public humiliation that for love of the country I had the fortitude to bear, despite the anger and mortification I felt at the thought that my own mother had wounded me, twice in fact, since not only had she had the incredible madness to have bought me that kind of Bike but she never even realized the offense she goes on and persists in committing against my natural self-respect. In spite of that, already way beyond the limits of the inexcusable, every day I ped-aled very high above all affects and pettiness, for my desire was nonetheless stronger than the stings of hurt pride. But you on the other hand took the opposite tack, when you didn't even have to overcome the double chagrin of having been betrayed by your mother and having to face the mocking looks of every kid in the neighborhood. Which by the way pushed me to excel at Biking. You, the minute the Bike turned up, the first day of the Bike I saw you retreat even further into the house into the depths of your room, which you almost never came out of, digging yourself a burrow or a den if you prefer in your handful of books, and from that day and during those final years all you ever did was work, work, I told myself and not live and I from the vantage point of the Bike I knew I was soaring over the Clos-Salembier and our common and respective chains. And Algeria I knew it.

And uttering these words my brother sitting under my eyes *is* the child flown off on his bike, I see he's it, such is the power of childhood and of the Bike, clearly he emerges from memory and enters before me with a great crash of wheels on the balcony.

My turn now, I was thinking. Not that my brother got it wrong. But he has just accused me of very real deeds of which I am not, I was thinking, the author but the victim. The Bike's role in our destinies cannot be de-nied, but it is not at all what he thinks. Everything or almost in my brother's story can be related to the initial trauma of the Bike's arrival, of that I am sole witness. *Le* sole witness? No. *La* sole witness? The soul sister and witness and loving nonetheless, I pray the language will take me where I want us to go. For all this was done to surprise us and then undone be-cause he was my brother of sister hand-in-hand and I was the sister of his heart and mind. Without my worries about how he'd end up and his about what might happen to me one of us would be dead more or less. Later they will even be able to say, if nothing new comes along, that the soul of my brother was marked indelibly by what became the Bike affair for him and thus obliquely for me insofar as I was on his side as a brother (but on the other side the sister that I am is on my mother's side). By a quasi symmetry the Bike wreaked havoc in my existence too, I see it still the bicycle which to my eyes was ravishing, with its little blue bodice. But the relationship between the Bike and me is not at all what my brother may or may wish to believe. My turn, I say. I start the Bike up from scratch again. I do not deny that I did not use the Bike, even though my mother, objectively betraying my brother's nature in favor of mine but without realizing this subjectively, had shown her interest in seeing me become a Biker.

I do not deny that not having taken advantage of the extraordinary opening on the world that the Bike held I did not in fact get to know Algeria, while maintaining that I never stopped dreaming of exploration and discovery right up to the day of the Bike's arrival. For my brother as for me, the Bike's entry was a turning point in our inner lives, but in opposite directions. And if there was a turn, hence very big event it is because of what this Bike, later known as the Bike, the one and only, had taken, in the way of importance, necessity, and promises, to its slender frame before it made its appearance. And before going on, let me emphasize that this particular Bike was in fact an apparition, not merely a bike, perhaps *the apparition* for us both.

Because there it was at last, after having been awaited four years which at our young age was more like twelve or eternity, and in the meantime we had become the champion Bike-awaiters, champion ghost cyclists, so racked by our need that we were sick over it because otherwise we'd have become criminals, and it was an antimaternal sickness, a furtive shameful resentment, turned against ourselves with respect to our mother and Omi our maternal grandmother, who, for reasons not entirely clear didn't respond to our desire for four which is to say twelve years, although on every possible occasion we voiced the same wish, the minute it was logically permissible to imagine it coming we were on the alert but respectfully, for all this had commenced shortly after the death of my father and we sincerely observed the period of mourning. The nonaccomplishment of our wishes seemed a mysterious sequel to our father's irreversible disappearance: now we had come in touch with the impossible, we had come in contact with the irreparable, there are prayers that are not answered, the Bike didn't come, as my father didn't come; something prevented my mother from granting our wishes however desperate and I didn't see what, no doubt perhaps it was the size of the expense of a real Bike compared with more immediate needs mostly food, or maybe a secret obstacle of which one couldn't speak and whose hypothetical existence softened the intensity of our pleadings, day and night we prowled on velvet paws at the base of the maternal wall, ceaselessly expressing but in a contained way but with every inch of our bodies our request for the absolute Object. We pretended to have a bike, we acted a play called First Race, we mimed the champion and the Bike itself. And there was no refusal. No letter of rejection. That got our hopes up. At each birthday and each Jewish holiday naturally we expected it, that is, four or five times a year, we thought only of it each day brought us closer to its proximity. Bike need and vital hope occasionally drove us crazy. Of the Bike craze was born the necessity for the rites of a religion to which otherwise, Bike aside, we had been neither initiated nor attached, but the urgency made us join hands and bow our heads, the incontestably vital urgency of the Bike for both of us made us convert to our own religion which we barely knew—since we had to believe, believe or burst, believe that a miracle could happen—and that's how the Bike, grasped in its promise but without a word, drifting in our dreams like a two-wheeled kite that my brother saw shimmering clearly and that I, plunged in a myopic haze saw only as an iridescent reflection in my brother's strangely liquid pupils, that's how the Bike brought us to our knees.

But at each occasion, therefore twelve or fifteen times in a row, no bike comes and no explanation. And no refusal. It doesn't come. It hasn't come. Shocked, my brother and I clung to one another, compassion unites us more strongly than ever, each understands the chagrin and disappointment of the other. It doesn't come, it doesn't come, it doesn't come, and that's how a bike becomes everything for us, by a record of notcoming. I shall not speak of the sheer obliviousness of my grandmother during these years, better to say nothing. They didn't realize. And that modifies the family structure, we are two against two, without their seeming concerned about this. I shall not speak of the shock of the sweater knit secretly in shades of pale blue and chick yellow wool the famous surprise announced by my grandmother for one of my birthdays and that made us shudder with joy for three months, since there could be only one surprise in the world. I shall speak of this state close to revolt, this dim state into which we plunge hand in hand, and of the dizzying abyss which opened between them and us. All this was inside the house.

But outside we became a family again, to fend off a variety of attacks from the enemy camps, thanks to which we were forced to keep from falling apart. When my mother returned bruised from the City of Algiers, having been mistreated as a widow, our anger vanished, a truce of the Bike in truth we thought only of Mother, oh! if I had a bike thought my brother immediately, up on his high horse, downtown, I would promptly have laid low such and such an adversary and me too I thought this, but we are so removed from the scene where our mother, far from her allies, does battle alone and is almost always unhorsed by her youth and honesty.

Whereupon, against all expectations, it appears. The Bike. What a shock! Totally unforeseen. Fatal.

We continued to believe in "heaven," that was our mistake, given that heaven means: a tomb on your head. A tomb or a bomb or a crate of vegetables. On your head. That's hell for you: the crate of heaven that lands on your head, just when you look up thinking the time has come for you to fly. For your birthday. Heaven landed on both of us but each receives it according to his nature, his sex, his temperament, on the head. Suddenly, in the dining room, unveiled: the Bike. Not there one minute, there the next. The Bike jumps, the Bike bursts into pieces, the miracle in smithereens on the floor.

I see my brother rampage into the garden breathing fire trampling everything under his hoofs he lifts the bicycle, throws it to the ground and yells: I'm leaving!

—You're leaving! I cried out.

—A girl's bike! What an insult! I won't stay here another second he yells.

—I'm coming with you I shouted. I run, I'm scared he's going to jump on the Bike, that he's going to ride like a madman to Wild Woman Ravine, that he's going to ride up without slowing down on the contrary right up to the edge of the Ravine, that he's going to drop like a stone tangled up in the Bike headfirst, his little legs thrashing the air to climb back up too late, I holler Pierre! Pierre! A nightmare. It's the Wild Woman Ravine nightmare. It comes back to me now as if it were yesterday how my little brother drops like a stone. All you see of him are his two little arms of convulsed legs rising toward the sky, a half-crushed petrified prayer.

My brother yells: she insulted me! She's killed me again! My brother grabs the iron rod. I cry: Stay! My grandmother calls very loud in German *Solch ein Kukuch nochmal!* It's her sharpest cry of indignation. She calls us cuckoos or rather *Koukous,* Pierre me the Bike *Koukous.* We koukareer off, with the Bike that follows us or accompanies us I don't know how, we koukareer to our end no doubt about that.

Behind us, the two small silhouettes of the bewildered goddesses eyes dazed. My mother has one eye bulging, hair on end. Omi is laughing. Omi laughs. In anger or in fright. My brother brandishes the iron rod. Under the shock of the apparition, I moan, darkness falls over my life as a sister, I sway, I slither down the stairs of my first tragedy, this therefore is where it begins all the misfortune that will dog us, here is a fault, a crime, a lesion a black cloud over our faces. I run I whimper behind my brother "Forever I am going away!" "Go I'll follow you. To prevent you, I'll hang onto your shirt, your shorts!" There we are in the great dust of the world, heading for destruction, my iron brother me at his heels. Had I known! says regret and each in his own cracked mind hears the deplorable sentence groan in the iron.

—I'm fucking nice the whole year! And she spits on me! my brother bursts out.

I draw a veil over it, I blur, I swear he said: I do my utmost to be nice, she gives me a stick or maybe a spritz. I pray neither the gods nor the neighbors hear.

—Staggering from the blow of this Bike on my head exclaims my brother I see the future I see it all and it will always be forever. I see Mummy do it again. Her whole life! Her whole life! I see all the blows she will be giving me for never once having had a good look at me. Ten years from now the same scene! Thirty years from now the same scene! Everything screwed up! If I had a tree to fell now, I would bring my iron rod down on the oak, *die Eiche,* under the eyes of Mummy-and-Omi I would hack it to pieces through the middle, thought my brother aloud and with such feeling that I could see the scene in all its details. All by himself with the iron rod a yard and a half long lying around the garden like an invitation. He makes the silhouette call out, the trunk yield, as only a man who is all worked up can to show Mummy-and-Omi the two little goddesses in over their depth he is showing them what he can do. The trees in the garden being my father's trees, he doesn't touch them.

I fell the oak he foams, licking his chops. Or if I had a rat! Horror! a little rat skips out in front of us as if ordered up in replacement by Anon., author of our nightmares. I shout already the iron clangs down. The rat pretty much hacked in two barely squirms on the ground, or perhaps reached by the number and pitch of my screams in the cavern that rage has dug in his secret life, my brother wavers, is moved, thinks it over, I scream louder and louder I am making myself deaf, the rat lifts its missile of a muzzle toward the sky and scrams. Immediately I am struck by the horrible thought that it might perhaps have been better if the rat had died for us. It might have averted the slaughter of a mother. One blood for another. But in the state I'm in I've broken the metonymy chain. I lose track. I'm getting carried away by the here and now. I do not think. I do not glimpse the cruel subtleties of sacrificial logic, I come to the defense of anything and everything I tell myself years later. But beneath the Bike's wheels a whirlwind of thoughts in every head events badly begun overtake us, from the instant the Bike is unveiled there is no halt to the killing mill, I see the four of us spinning like a family of flies in a funnel. What grandeur and what pettiness.

His whole life. His whole life.

He stomps in the road. He rips at the doors. She says: But it is a very good-looking German bicycle. I say: it is German. He says: she is abnormal. He says: you know the milk of motherly kindness, there's no such thing. Men: she knows nothing about them. A woman's bike in the Clos-Salembier! My enemies are going to crack up laughing. I'm leaving. Stay I pleaded exhaling all the care in the world. No way. Today that's it. Finished. He says: when I am sixty-five years old I'll still be thinking about it, just like today, just like today. I'll say: Mummy was out of her mind. Mummy is an old fool! A hundred years from now I'll still be saying it. Such are the words we have been using since we were small: "an old fool." Is there greater blasphemy in the world? Those are magic words, and when she is old as the world we'll still be saying them.

— Giving a girl's bike to your son, cries my brother is a crime. And in my opinion, he shouts, *the definitive crime.* Says he. There's a word that jingles in our poisoned purse. De-fin-i-tive. And in my opinion: definitive. Repeats my brother chopping it up. And why not a dress while you're at it, he cries, and at these words acid tears spray from his lids.— She amputates me, and she is amputated. Am-pute he adds ecstatically to the purse. Amputate! And in seventy years—amputated! She has amputated me of something definitive!

This Bike, says my brother, is a basic act of death. Today I remember it still as if it were seventy years ago, that's what I'll be saying seventy years from now, remember what I'm telling you he orders. And, indeed, I do remember. And now, farewell. Don't go I begged. Today it's over. Finished. She needs to be taught a lesson. She is killing me. She's got to understand, sacrificing me in the Clos-Salembier! the Arabs are going to have a good laugh. When she's eighty-seven years old she still won't have learned. And the bread. She buys two loaves of bread, the good one for you the bad for me. That's Omi, I say, the two loaves, but for her one is salted, the other sweet. It's all the same. You think I'm nuts? They are verging on madness. And what they're verging on those two is my suicide.

Then he took his anger and left pounding the earth underfoot and me I ran along whimpering between his great wild paws.

Then my mother said: if that's how it is, I won't have dinner. I won't sit down. Omi cried *Zum Kukuk nochmal* and stomped her left foot. A great indignation whirled them away and they left huffing and puffing in the astonished dusk.

The next day back comes my brother to the gate. I'm wondering if I should come back he says because I don't want Mummy to be all upset. Around him five ragged little snot-nosed kids. Is she upset? says my brother. Come back, I say. But if she isn't upset says my brother, I'm not coming back. The snot-nosed chorus at the bars of the gate. I can see by my brother's hair that last night he got to know Algeria.— Come back, I say.— So therefore she's upset? thinks my brother.— Certainly, beyond a doubt, I thought. We looked at one another. Between us the gate, impossible. I am miserable. I am miserable. I am my brother on the other side. Together we push slowly on the gate. The bunch of kids comes unstuck. The impossible gate comes between us, again, between us the children with two loaves and us the children without loaves. Without a word. My mother calls out: there's lots to eat. From the veranda. My brother comes back, for many opposite mixed-up reasons.

—But I didn't even buy it on sale! says my mother.

—Nothing ever becomes memory says my brother in the armchair. There is no such thing as forgetting. Just look at this Bike. There is no such thing as memory. It is a crime says my brother. It is total maternal incompetence says the pediatrician. It is the same always there is no such thing as time.

Whereas for me I thought everything that comes on stage shouting exits on paper.

—I have always wondered if there is *a Jewish woman in history* who on the day of her son's thirteenth birthday gives him a woman's bike.

My whole life I shall repeat it: when the time came for the symbol of the glory of manhood, and into the bargain in the Clos-Salembier, in front of all our chortling pint-sized-enemies, Mummy counted her pennies. My whole life, I shall emphasize the worst; Mummy *did not even want to castrate me.* Her whole life she took no notice of the man, nor the son, nor the woman, nor the mother. She picked up her little black bag and went to deliver a baby down in the Ravine when I was dying of pain.

I took the Bike, says my brother, and I mounted it. It weighed a ton.

—This bicycle story, says my scatterbrained mother he took it personally whereas *in truth* it was my sense of economy, I know, I say, because anyone could ride that bicycle and God knows what people used to ride in those days, all it had to do was roll, says my mother, and my children always held whatever I did against me and into the bargain all the things I didn't do without any sense of economy.

And furthermore I used that bike only once and never again afterwards. And furthermore I never ate the good bread, it's my brother who ate all the bread the Bike good or bad. And furthermore that Bike began to come between us, despite him despite me, that Bike bought to be one-bike-for-two with a slight preference for me became my brother's runaway Bike, day after day he soars off on it, a sublime kite with a long ribbon of snotty rags for a tail. All my mother's plans for naught, she would have done better to have bought a man's bike instead of buying a German two-wheeler but in her scatterbrained fashion she never realized there was a war going on in the Clos-Salembier in addition to the other wars in which we were embroiled, for we had to do battle all at once on several fronts, from behind and head on and off to one side under the arm eyeball-to-eyeball, swing round to fight off now a general onslaught, now a local attack or one on the left, the battlefields more or less vast occasionally cramped but as one conflict was always in touch with a neighboring hatred each shock sent its waves from top to bottom of the City of Algiers.

This City that people from all over describe as another one of those Cities renowned for their beauty and numerous pleasure spots, and which therefore could have been inhabited like a Venice or a Rome, and which was in fact idolized and monumentalized, this City of many names, like the divine Cities whose attributes one recites, for me it is Hell and precisely because of its abundance of delights, because of its heady streets, the twisty stinking little dark streets like the great long proud central ones, precisely because of the tumultuous, noisy, jostling, nonchalant intensity of its arcades its flights of stairs its cafés its fig trees laden with birds, its populations composed entirely of individuals rendered profound by their close calls with death, precisely because it was so elaborately deceitful and deceptive, while seeming to be life itself, whereas in reality as far as I could see it was war upon war, a scaffold of hostilities, a gigantic poisoned layer cake, lots of people are content and go to church, similarly they go to theater galas and similarly to certain beaches and not others, which was not our case, for we the Clos-Salembier family were not among the happy in church, but for me the City of Algiers is a lie and a wildly successful piece of skulduggery, a giant motley eggcup in the shape of a hen which broods on the eggs of war. In my opinion you cannot take a step in the street or enter a store without being instantly victim partner in crime guilty party or contaminated. Right away someone is busy corrupting someone busy crushing someone or someone busy watching you flee some unbearable human spectacle. According to my mother Germany is incurable, according to me the City of Algiers as crowning point and metaphor for all of Algeria is the incurable one. When I used to live in the heights of Hell in the Clos-Salembier, on the crest of Crest Road, I'd wonder if my mother was aware she had gone from a mortal scene to a scene of death, but according to my brother my mother never took any account of the quantity of mortal elements the City heaped up.

The Clinic might explain this: right smack in the, as I thought, sordid middle of the City prey in its entirety to knives imaginary and real, there it was, an enclave established by my father initially and after his death by my mother: the Cradle. At the very heart of war, the haven. And indeed the Clinic is protohistory itself. One came here naked to be born naked. The one and only place and time in which humanity has no other goal but to come, what an idea, out into the light of day. In the labor room, the world has only to be born. The best of Algeria as far as I could see had lived in this little room. Besides already, leaving the delivery room and taking a few steps toward the kitchen, a bit of war collected, smoldered, was batted out with some old rags and sometimes flared up again, but still never took over the whole of the terrain. On the other hand once you got to the door, that was it: everything, the whole kit and caboodle, mined, starting with the elevator, source of so much misery (I'll get to this later) then the building's corridor where the concierge, aided and abetted by my mother, blind to mortal danger, had opened an undergarments shop for pregnant women, and next the concierge's lodging which is nothing but a time bomb, planted with my mother's help in the basement of the building and which finally exploded, causing the devastation of the entire house, the disappearance lock, stock, and barrel of the Clinic and as a logical consequence, albeit unforeseen by the concierge, the destruction of the underwear shop for pregnant women panties and bras and the abrupt passage from prosperity to bankruptcy of those who had been counting on a rise in their fortunes.

But before the destruction and final annihilation of the Clinic in 1971, and therefore this terrible end which bears me out in every detail, anyone can be mistaken, between the deliveries and the howls, and as long as the babies continued to be born, it was an ongoing labor for life, not its opposite.

While we who were perched on a tree or on the roof of the Clos-Salembier from 1946 to 1956 saw everything that my mother in her nest below did not see.

On top of your basic French racism, racism as root reason foundation stone pillar society culture custom, on top of this triumphant congenital inoculation, this graft which could scarcely have better taken and be more widespread in the world, on top of French classicism, on top of this morbidity considered to be the very picture of health and a hearty appetite, you must put the various anti-Semitisms, which naturally add up between them: the anti-Semitism of each part of the whole with regard to the Jews (French Algerian French Spanish Arabs Corsican doctors civil servants lawyers) not to mention the Kabyles and the communists often themselves once Jews, the chronic anti-Semitism which my mother and Omi used to liken to the *gesunder Antisemitismus* they had put up with in Germany without its being too bothersome, and above and beyond your day-to-day anti-Semitism, the acute, very dangerous outbreaks of anti-Semitism; and above all, the antiwidowism that showed its face after my father died, among our relations, among my father's friends who all now aspired to be my mother's lovers or woe betide her and their wives who all without exception gave my mother and the family a cold shoulder, as a preventive measure,

furthermore in the Clos-Salembier there was war between the sexes brutal crude war like the War of the Roses a matter of thorns and of roses war between the scorched sexes, animals half-flayed, cats and rats whole or in pieces flung at one another, a war of child monsters that the adult superpowers turned a blind eye to, supplied with perversity or apparent indifference, but did not directly intervene in; a war on two fronts, on the one hand the war between the boys, same sex against same sex, it must be emphasized for this was among the circumcised, and was a matter of comparing erections, sticks, rods, fists, fingers, balls, pricks, dicks, biceps, and badges; on the other hand the war of the same against the others, where I was mostly on my own sisterless brotherless and friendless. With my grandmothers off in the kitchen, making an appearance at the end to collect the wounded, once the damage was done. Now I am the only one who can talk about this double war for I alone in the Clos-Salembier was on both sides, as brother on my brother's side and as girl without my brother who in this case could never have been my sister. I know what defilement is. However the greatest suffering is not the defilement that on several occasions brought me to the brink of suicide.

The most intolerable, above and beyond the battles and humiliations, is that we were assailed in the Clos-Salembier by those whom we wanted to love, with whom we were lamentably in love, to whom we were attached we thought by kinship and communities of origin, by destiny, by our manner of thinking, by memory, by touch, by taste, our enemies were our friends, there was error and confusion on the side on all the sides I wanted to be on their side but it was a desire on my side on their side the desire had no side, it had no here, it was burning coals a thornbush of arms, I only wanted their City and their Algeria, with all my strength I wanted to arrive there I could spend hours squatting a few yards away from them without moving, hoping to demonstrate my goodwill, a kind of patience and behavior that I never had with the French camp, the minute there was French I was exultation arms where there were Arabs I was hope and wound. Me, I thought I am *inseparab*. This is an unlivable relationship with oneself.

By which I mean those whom we called the "kidzArabs," dimly persuaded as we were of having been since birth and before destined to one another and separated as happens in Grimm's fairy tales, we felt like ugly ducklings but promised redress, and we cited, my brother and I as prefiguration that last trip we made with my father in 1948 in the Citroën, leaving from the Clinic passing in front of the Main Post Office rumbling down to the bottom of Algiers's famous hills, and it was at the beginning of Crest Road that my father stopped the Citroën to pick up two hitchhiking Arabs. This, you understand, was absolutely unheard of in those days. All the more so as one could not be sure the Citroën would start up again. You have to tickle its nose for a long while with the crank. In the Citroën an unforgettable fiesta the two passengers thanking us exuberantly for the unexpected hospitality, how right they were to believe in and hope for that which one cannot reasonably count on, the world is better than one thinks, look, a Frenchman stopped for them which is an error I think my father is not French although he may believe he is, my father is an anomaly in the history of this country, it is on the one hand as a piece of detritus spit out rejected by the French and on the other hand as my ideal of a doctor living like a loony in the Clos-Salembier where no normal doctor which is to say one equipped with normal medical financial professional ambitions would have set up shop, in this neighborhood with no French inhabitants not fit for success not fit for a social life, it is therefore, I repeat, as a peculiar kind of Arab that my father an arabizarre has stopped, knowing as he did so that the Citroën once reined up was always difficult to get going again, and also not a dozen days before his death of which he had or didn't have a presentiment, which we shall never know, but this we mustn't tell our two passengers—that my father is really an Arab beneath the facade of young and dashing French doctor, being Jewish what's more, which could tip the scales either way—for this would deprive our two enchanted guests of the marvelous feeling that in this sick and cursed with hatred and totally impossible country, in spite of everything, anything could happen. When we reached the corner of Laurent-Pichat Boulevard my father stopped the car at the top of the hill and our two humans transfigured at the same time as my father my brother and me, got out, hearts agape, the door, the door, saying thank you you are a brother thank you my brother god bless you brother in French and in exchange my father says that they are his brothers in Arabic. Still today we speak of this final occasion with high naïveté, all our dreams coming true a few days before the final closing of the doors. But the greatest piece of luck is that we had actually been in the Citroën climbing back up from the depths of Algiers toward the Clos-Salembier, something that never happened to us. Ever since each year we retell the story about when the doors of heaven were thrown open before us at the corner of the boulevard, how my father having been named brother we were children of brother for a few days. The sky was naturally intensely blue, the teeth of our smiles brilliantly white, our companions biblical, and thereupon god is dead and the book of doors slams shut in our faces.

My brother claims the two men were not hitchhiking, it doesn't make sense he says, who but my father would have stopped on Crest Road and my father is an ephemeral being, who stopped all by himself, he was forever stopping all by himself says my brother he liked to pick people who hadn't asked for anything up in his Citroën. He had the human touch. Says my brother in the year 2000. We liked the Citroën and its name, we believed we could hear it bloom *citron* and *troëne*—lemon and privet hedge—right up to the day when going by in the other direction I saw it choking from living in that land of hate. The two men were oldsters in gandouras, who were waiting at the stop to flag down the trolley and they were going down says my brother, down into Algiers, they were not even going up.

I never had a bit of luck, no matter how hard I tried. I searched I didn't find. I started again from the beginning, the whole time I was living in Algeria, I tried-all-the-same.

Everything that moves in me everything that gets itself going and runs after, and therefore writing may be traced back to Oran's doors in the first instance and later to the various doors of Algiers, it seems as if I am always being taken back to the invisible doors of the quite different cities of Oran then Algiers, and especially to their invisibility source of my constant misadventures inasmuch as not seeing them I banged up against them or I was banged against them, in any case I could feel them the way a blind person feels bars and gates advancing to meet him, and moves with his hair on end saying "I see a gate, I see a grill" always using the word *see* for what she doesn't see with her eyes but that she sees with everything that takes the place of eyes, presentiment, breathing, the heart's ears, all the other organs endowed with seeing, and the fingertips.

City moreover has always meant to me one hundred doors besieged besieging City enclosure entrenched camp barbed wire enceinte Clos-Salembier niche enclave captivity exits troy oran algiers man blood and woman blood without me

whereas Paris no, Paris is doorlesss and therefore without opposing forces without pleading without assault without horse without dog and City I do not live it as

the difference between Oran and Algiers is sexual, Oran was woman to me and Algiers the man, in Oran I acted the woman, in Algiers the man, because of the way the City of Oran was as I thought all seduction round rose spicy in the armpits, all flight, I ran after it, she all veils, veils, mutinous, vivacious, flighty, me forever losing my way, lost in the mauve vapors of the Turkish bath, lover fondling the endless bodies of my dissolved relatives

whereas Algiers was bite the dust, straddle, fall from a great height, with or without brother or father, dust myself off and try again. In the Clos-Salembier I wanted to take Algeria by force, I reached the end, everything started spinning, and that is when I became haunted by the dead and all unawares, I was gripped by a kind of frenzy, like a ghost with only a few hours till day breaks and puts a halt to its attempt to transgress,

I was going faster and faster, and not necessarily ahead, only at top speed, I didn't realize immediately that I wasn't getting there, I didn't realize either that I would not get there.

On one side I was attacking on the other I was fighting back, I was going so fast, so blindly, that often like the wild horses in *Macbeth* I eat myself. At five thirty in the morning a little cock crowed in the distance. It struck the far-off note.

I take the Bike. There had been: the Dog. We had awaited its coming with the veneration due to the Dog foretold by our father, the Annunciation Dog, our brother and child. And now the Dog who was once the king and son of God is slowly descending into disinheritance, a flop of a life locked up in the cage.

But whatever his beginning his end his miserable destiny, there is only one dog and it is the Dog. And the Dog is ourselves like it or not, ourselves for better or for worse as we shall see.

And now there is: the Bike. And whatever the future may hold in store there will be no other Bike than this one, not the German bicycle but it itself. We say: the Bike, and my brother and I see the Clos-Salembier and the origin of our family cycle again, though there may be dozens of bikes between the Bike and us, especially on my brother's side. The Bike remains, absolute, not very tall, its armor pale blue and all the more virile in the end as it was feminine at the outset. This Bike was our lot: to my brother it gives Algeria, from the very day after the famous day, to me: nothing. From the very start it stressed my absence from the world that I wanted more than anything in the world.

I take the bike. Four years of waiting come undone. You know how you forget all the pain once it comes? I glide down the drive. I am outside. I take Morning Glory Street. And that's when the vegetable crate comes flying at the wheel my knee my heart. The Bike—the crate the fated pair. The kids crack up. The kids piss. I should have kept going. But no: I saw the future. There was none.

From then on I renounced the Bike. What I can bear on foot without giving in, the rough and tumble, the clinches full of hatred, rolling on the gravel, I cannot bear in the state of Bike. This is a fact that I am capable of analyzing today but not before. I am much stronger on foot, I tell myself, stronger morally and therefore physically, I am stronger one-to-one between equals in the hatred and the rubbish but from higher up I am morally weak, higher up and therefore lower down, richer and therefore less equal and more questionable and therefore obviously weaker physically. If I had been my brother I would have grabbed the iron bar, or died of shame. But I didn't dare.

I was already a patchwork of scars, I had the gate scar, the Fips scar, the blue morning glory scar, the hopscotch scar, each time a violent opening of the body, once a scratch in my right eye, once five gaping stars in my left foot, once the hole of the stake in my right thigh just beside the femoral artery. Falling off the bike doesn't leave a scar but it takes the outside back. A hole in the dreams I had been dreaming for four years. But the bike plus vegetable crate, I tell myself is the opposite of the winged Bike. It is not my vision of the world. I renounce. Inversely my brother inadvertently betrayed by my mother with Omi leaves for Algeria despite the humiliation or because of it. That bike really drove a wedge between us, I thought, up to then we were just one brother with an internal sister and vice versa now I was nothing but a sister with no internal brother, and as my brother says I for my part burrowed deeper and deeper into *my solitary reveries.*

My mother—not to mention Omi, who never learned to ride a bike—could not grasp the necessity of the Bike which was for us the Liberty Horse, as well as the humble but fabulous offspring of the Citroën the beloved automobile that my mother had sold to a City of Algiers vegetable dealer a sale which cost us our soul and a topic on which we all held our peace, that silence one wraps around the intolerable wounds grief inflicts on the vanquished, and to which orphans are forced to submit, without their consent. We never brought the subject up. But we thought of it and its new life which, as we could not admit, tormented us with shame and remorse, the life of a noble beast sold for a beast of burden, forever filthy and crammed with vegetables. My mother belonged to a different order of necessity. The Bike was nothing for her for us it was everything. She was incapable of seeing that it was the Life-Thing, the Key-Thing, the Sent-Thing, the sliding door to Algeria that is to the world we did not yet wish to renounce, first of all because she was the very picture of German health which prevented her imagining the very real suffering of Algerian invalids such as us, illness has always been lacking in my mother and madness even more so, since to this day she thinks that *illness is a kind of madness,* a mental deviation from normality, a poor psychological attitude, a failure to stand up straight. Never has she had the least sympathy or indulgence for the so-called ill who what's more abound in my father's family and whom she has always looked after with the clockwork and unswerving faithfulness to one's post of the healthy. And then: because she has always been free to come and go in Algeria, unlike us, no one has ever managed to deprive her of the freedom she brought with her from Germany, even when she herself was abandoned, left with Omi-for-world, rejected by the so-called community of my father's friends who thought of her exclusively as a piece of meat under the jurisdiction of my father's body, or after the husband's death, part and parcel of their own plate, a fate which was so foreign to my mother's way of thinking that overnight she found doors slammed in her face, as happens to all young widows in all underdeveloped countries, but not in Germany. And even when she found herself cast out, quarantined for good at the age of thirty-six, all the doors of hospitality and friendship bolted from within, by a shameless violence which at least made the children we were champions of the precocious analysis of the family conjugal adulterous inhospitable craven repugnant to our eyes society, but my mother indifferent, in good health blooming even, and furthermore armor-plated by the state of emergency and by her German genetic heritage as the daughter of a German war widow, without losing a second made her way to the Hospital, the very one where, without trembling without it even crossing her mind that she could tremble in that place, the very place where my father her husband had died, and signs up to become a midwife. With her astounding aptitude for recovery. Remove her tree and she bounds to the top of the next one. And from there, from the Hospital she can now call hers, before four years have passed she creates the new world, one hundred percent hers owing nothing to anyone, or even to my father unless to his death which is the reason for my mother's new life. While the beloved automobile for its part, ssh, sold off brought low my mother freer than ever rises. And where, may we ask? In the very heart of this Algerian fecundity, which we, I especially, have been dreaming of since the days when I used to walk in order to be within reach at last of the body, the arms, the breasts, the hands. Even in prison, she found a kind of freedom, since despite being locked up, once the first couple of nights during which she says she couldn't catch a wink for the noise had passed, once she was settled in the cell, with the other four ladies, she slept all the better on her sack of straw for being in prison. At least during this time, she tells me, a little embarrassed a shameful thing she couldn't tell a soul but me, she doesn't have to worry about the Clinic weighing her down like a burden and a prison, something she'd rather didn't get around, for she feels a little dishonest in spite of herself. And the reason is that she benefited from prison, which in principle one is not only not supposed to benefit from but to suffer from in a hundred different ways whereas my mother with her freedom and her German aptitude for adaptation, without meaning to had been unable to keep herself from benefiting in all sorts of ways and particularly in the acquisition of a freedom which needless to say had never crossed her mind when at the drop of a hat they shipped her off.

While for my brother, finding himself in the same prison, because of my mother, but on the men's side, prison was Hell, and in all kinds of ways, beginning naturally with the brutal and unjust loss of liberty, an exalting loss and an exalting brutality, says my brother, and similarly an exalting Hell, and therefore a rising descent, just like Dante's rising descent says my brother, in the same prison but on the side of the "queers," it was a prodigious and formative adventure, of prodigious power, as all those who have had the terrifying luck to ascend by the downward path know, I've been fortunate all my life says my brother, thanks to mother I have even escaped a life without prison, I did battle with myself for twenty-four days and in the end I was the absolute winner, I beat myself off, I scrunched myself up small and got the better of myself whereas my mother with her preexisting and unfailing absolute sense of freedom never had to do battle with herself, in prison she was like a fish.

While mother, says my brother, has always been an amputee, suffering from not suffering stricken with a-madness which is the sickness of those who do not know what sickness is.

No, my mother, in structural terms, was not built to understand the gravity of the Bike business, she did not see, structurally, that we were crazed and ill with our need of Algeria, with the inner reality of the country that was the country of our birth and not ours at all, from the flesh, from the habitat, from the Arabness of the Arabitude, from the treasure full of treasures to which we had no access, lacking which we made it up knowing full well that we were only drawing the outlines of ghosts. My mother was contented with a tiny but central part, where she soon managed to bring three or four hundred Algerian babies into the world each year. A beautiful thing, but for us another heartache for there was no follow-up: once born in the Clinic, thus in our house, all these children entered Algeria while we who were born there, but not in the Clinic, didn't go with them, we were not allowed in. In any case so long as the French held Algeria. In any case so long as due to a fatal and indissoluble misunderstanding, we were screened and rejected as "French." After-the-French, the doors began to open, including the prison door, and my mother entered, followed by my brother, but I was no longer there.

But my industrious mother who rebuilt her nest every time in exile, in the very fork of exile, could not fathom that we should want at all cost to enter and arrive in a country; that we were sick with love, whereas she had known and been through exiles exclusions expulsions exactions without ever getting sick and especially not with love, she hates sickness and most of all the sickness of love, the minute she sees any sign of illness, she drives it away in horror, which is perhaps why having found the frenzy of our longing for the Bike suspect, she held out against us for four years like a veritable madwoman in our opinion involuntarily denying us mental health while believing she was hardening us. A tie she thinks is made to be broken, a desire to be cut off. I wonder, my brother wonders, if she didn't become a midwife out of an innate or acquired tendency to cut cords. The two German sisters my aunt Eri and my mother both in effect learned cutting, then the one took up sewing and the other my mother according to my brother, the cutting of cords. But I think it is her love of a job well done that pointed her in the direction of the supreme job of work carried out in the labor room. At her place, the Clinic, there were no dead women. Nor illnesses. Two things I never saw, says my mother: an infected cord; I never saw a case of phlebitis at the Clinic either.

—Expulsion, says my mother, is when the head comes out, and the rest pops out after all by itself.

If the woman was doing well, she got down from the table five minutes after giving birth, she walked to her room and never any hemorrhaging, my mother bursts out. Whereas at the hospital they had this stupid rule of not letting the women move, the hospital invented the fear of hemorrhaging. But the Moors who used to give birth at home had known for ages about getting up. In the Clinic we got up right away, and it was a big party with the Staff as opposed to those stupid French hospitals which turned it into a way of being sick. The Moors and I were always up and about early. In the stupid hospital a person who went into labor wasn't supposed to budge the doctors said, says my mother blowing on her ancient rage then still young and fresh to shine it up again, forced into bed, forced onto the labor table she had to be tied up and if she is still struggling put her to sleep, strap them down I never forgot that later the person in labor who wants to walk, strapped down, so many errors and so much change, after she had given birth she had to lie flat on her belly for two hours, and naturally people begin by making mistakes, in order to change things mistakes must be made. But at the Clinic if the person wants to walk she walks and never a drop of blood during labor, between the doctors who are not human, the doctors who are not qualified, the doctors who are qualified but who are dying of fear, there were still a few midwives to keep people calm especially the terrified new mothers.

If I had time I'd tell you the story of the qualified doctor who always arrived too late because of the curfew, you had to call an ambulance to take him to the customer in labor five minutes' walk away, but because of the curfew the ambulance arrived too late or never, but I don't have time says my mother, it's time for the Market, the place instinct unfailingly carries her back to. The Market is a must. By now it was raining so hard that a minimum of common sense ought to have kept her at home, but nobody'd dream of keeping her from the Market it is all that remains of her splendid creation swallowed up lock, stock, and barrel, the Market as forever rekindled vestige of the ruins of the Universe where my mother fleeing the stupidity of the hospital gave the person in labor liberty, walking.

Expulsion for my brother and me first of all, then for me alone after the Bike's parting of our ways, was the very form of our existence and relationship to the world from the Clos-Salembier house, and the direct, unfortunate, and originally totally unforeseen consequence of the various expulsions to which my father had been subjected right up to the moment in 1946 when in order to escape from those brutalities and their mnemonic effects, and no doubt with the idea of forgetting them and beginning a new life my father moved to Algiers that is as soon as possible after the war, thus leaving Vichy-in-Oran behind and flying on his own not suspecting for an instant that he was headed straight for his brutal expulsion from the world of the living, following which, the nest he had chosen to rear us in, thinking that we would enjoy having a garden and the closeness he and we had desired to a vast and extremely downtrodden but Algerian society, this place called Clos-Salembier on the death of my father became once again the site of multiple and endless expulsions. If only he had known. For what was perhaps possible under the wing of father husband man, which was to go in and out on both sides was utterly out of the question for a group that was lacking father husband man and especially in and from the Clos-Salembier. He had opened the Clinic down below, in town, the house was perched above and away from the City in a garden at the mouth of Wild Woman Ravine where tens of thousands of wretched people crowded together without water and without shelter, and that is where my father sets us down with the idea of having ties with Algerians.

—When Vichy arrived in Oran says my mother suddenly from one day to the next they told yourfather you cannot go on working as a doctor. And overnight he stopped. What am I going to do, he says, because there were people he was caring for, says my mother. So I said, says my mother, they can't stop me from treating people since I am not a doctor. Yourfather picked up a steak and a syringe. He took the needle and he showed me how to jab it straight into the steak you aspirate a little to make sure you are not in a vein, says my father to my mother, and a few years later my mother instructs me, then yourfather dropped me off in front of a lady's house. I went in. I am the nurse, I say, I have come for your shot, I say saysmymother, so you won't be afraid, do you mind lying down says she, and she lay down from then on I gave all your father's shots without a hitch. I myself, on the other hand, when I gave my midwife mother's shots, I was always in fear and trembling, I've never got over those shots, each time I gave a shot it was as if I committed a triple betrayal: betrayal of the patient to begin with, betrayal of her fear and trust, and then betrayal of my mother who never realized I had a problem with shots, I would never have said I am a nurse, because I've never been one, when a father, overcome by his little boy's terror, and the sight of the bare bottom of the child who was screaming with fear at the idea of the shot and the sight of the syringe I was holding, broke down and cried, half-crumpled up on Omi's sofa which I was using as an operating table, miming with all his soul the distress and tenderness of a parent in a tragedy, which only Algerians could do sincerely, I couldn't stop myself from trembling and feeling my soul soiled by a guilty horror, for I was afraid to miss the famous upper lateral quadrant, I was losing my grip on all medical knowledge of anatomy and if I could have thrown the syringe away every time and taken flight without jeopardizing my mother I would have done so. But I had the strength to run away only once, at the sight of a father who pleaded with me and clung to my knees instead of holding his son's as I had advised him when I saw the tiny bottom whose target I had to hit and every time I raised the syringe the man shouted no! not yet! each time no! not yet! till in the end the syringe grew big in my hand, I see the sword, I see the stage, I let it drop, I could not do otherwise, the father with child saved but betrayed, no shot and all my fault. The third betrayal was that of my father who died proud of me and whose confidence I betrayed posthumously. All the same until I-left-I-fled Algeria, I hold the syringe sin after sin, but immediately afterward I let it go. It may even be that the shot-problem further incited me to leave the country, one reason among many, but I would rather believe that this is impossible.

—The Red Cross telephoned to tell yourfather he was on night call when he hasn't the right to practice fine with them when the sirens start blowing if it's for the indigent population but it is out of the question yourfather says, and as a result after the war we were not allowed into Red Cross swimming pools.

The next day he met a colleague and told him I no longer have the right to practice, and the Christian tells him: Jew, you are crazy! Keep working and don't say anything, this friend told him: Jew! Just go on working. But he didn't dare, says my mother, nobody disobeyed those laws. Yourfather let himself be banned from practicing medicine, and when the Occupation ended I tell him I think you should continue doing podiatry since your health isn't very good but he says it distresses me not to practice medicine and when my husband went back to work I stopped giving shots, stupidly says my mother, do you realize says my mother that thanks to Vichy he was less tired and later unfortunately he went straight to death practicing medicine. My wisdom didn't always pay off says my mother with a well-tempered regret. In another way each time that I did a lot of good it backfired. Still you too were clever at things, you picked things up quickly and you were a good stand-in for the Clos-Salembier shots says my mother whose trust has always dissuaded me from owning up to my sins. Each time that I am about to admit my shameful suffering along with certain utterly scandalous and still vivid deeds I shut up. Not only have I betrayed the purity of her trust and her tendency to take me as a witness against my father by not saying anything so as not to deprive her of my support, which I have done my whole life and still do here today even, for I have no fear of her reading these pages, which are of no interest to her. But still I have always felt I was committing crimes against the very people whose good I so ardently desired, minimal crimes maybe, the size of a shot not done but a crime is a crime and the anguish I feel is forever sharp.

Yourfather never had *the idea of the Clos-Salembier* says my mother had I been consulted things would have turned out differently, coming from Oran yourfather did not know the Clos-Salembier. We only ended up in the Clos-Salembier by chance, a series of chances, which finally led us to the Clos-Salembier a place which at first glance greatly appealed to me. In life one does not always know how to jump at the opportunity. That's why we lived in the Clos-Salembier because yourfather didn't jump at the opportunities. As for me I never wanted to force things. Another error. In life one must also force things. Jump or force. We didn't do it when we should have, next yourfather died and I began to jump at the opportunities. The fact is that he really wanted to start a practice in Algiers. My father wanted happiness. Beauty. Grandeur. From 1945 until the move he painted and sang the City of Algiers to us, I saw visions of the City in gold and ivory in somber yews in fountains in art in gardens with my enchanted eyes through my father's hymns of praise, I *saw* the desired City and I still carry around inside me the last painting in which all the visions my father conjured up were radiantly fused. There was a superb villa right at the corner of Bru Boulevard with a view over the whole City, which nothing prevented us from having. He went there to rent it you have to make a deposit says the lady and yourfather has forgotten his checkbook. When he came back someone else had a checkbook there first. Chance again says my mother. The second house we didn't get had a garden with palm trees and also a wonderful view that I regretted but someone beat your father to it. The third house was the apartment adjoining the Clinic, a marvel right next door and up for sale, I thought that that would be extraordinary the apartment next to the Clinic. But your father refused to borrow. And that was his downfall. Because if I had been next door I could have kept an eye on what was going on inside and helped him, he could have leaned on me. Whereas in the Clos-Salembier we are far away, we see nothing, we know nothing. Plus after his death I could have had that apartment instead of being forced to live in two windowless rooms on the seventh floor. Whereupon yourfather remembered the last possibility and that was the Clos-Salembier, of which he had heard nothing until then. It was a matter of luck, but the fact is that yourfather didn't jump on the other houses and I coming from Germany I didn't want to force things.

In any case for the Clinic he dealt with a Jewish broker who, says my mother (although she's Jewish or maybe because she's Jewish) didn't help at all for the Philips equipment in 1946 he had to borrow everything.

In this villa which had been previously occupied by a military man, we found *the sabers.* In our opinion the sabers lay in wait for us as my father's scepters. My brother and I were convinced we would find proof of this idea on moving in. We opened the worm-eaten door of the stable and there are the sabers. Chance does nothing but obey our parents' most secret wishes I say, wishes kept secret from them too naturally, for otherwise they'd never have come true quite so precisely. One of them wishes for legend and to die, one of them hopes for freedom without ever having asked for it. We know it, we knew it, *in secret* I say. But my brother asks me to stick to the first person. In the battle between my parents, a battle undeclared, in which my brother the Dog and I were the most ardent hostages, each of them carried the day according to his soul and its destination. Coming from Oran, we, my brother and I, expected to find the sabers in the villa, I insisted. You are dreaming for two says my brother. But he doesn't ask for the dream to be suppressed.

What scared us the first evening says my mother is the infernal racket on the veranda. Yourfather took one of the sabers. It turned out to be cats in dry leaves.

We had robbers right away the second night. The first day Omi and I had hung some sheets up on the line in front of the kitchen and in the morning they were gone.

That never happened again, the third night yourfather having been summoned for an emergency in Wild Woman Ravine, even if he was no longer a general practitioner. From then on everything was fine.

The dead cats, remember, I say. Every month the dead cat, the cat of the month. A sudden stink would wake us up. An explosion. But the neighbor rushed around burying the dead cat in the garden and as soon as the body was covered with our soil the smell stopped like a cry cut off.

The flowerbed on the right, the one with dahlias and chrysanthemums, I say, broad beans, green beans, peas, says my brother, the flowerbed full of dead cats. The potatoes, tomatoes, radishes, peppers, zucchini, eggplant were on the other side.

To the right the gate, to the left of the Driveway.

Between us the gate. Us? I mean that other us that the gate began separuniting into those small daily agonies which are for us—my brother-what's-left-of-the-Dog-and-me-the-spirit-or-the-genius-of-the-Clos-Salembier—and for me the epitome of my Disalgeria.

In the beginning says my mother I believed that we lived next door to the Wild Woman Rabbi, another of those inexplicable strokes of luck.

The bike and the dog are the Clos-Salembier's signs I told myself. Now that my thoughts keep returning to the Clos-Salembier a place I haven't been back to in forty years and where, I told myself, I shall never go again, what do I see shining with a melancholy gleam in the polished black of the sky above the garden? The Bike and the Dog. I went away forty years ago and even in my thoughts I no longer return, I thought sitting on the balcony of the house which has taken the place of the Clos-Salembier house and all of a sudden, forty years later, I notice that my house reminds me of the Clos-Salembier house it's the veranda, it's the same drive as the Driveway, it's the gate, I'd never noticed this before, it's the same exactly but without the Dog without the Bike without father without mother without children, it's the shadow of itself and I'd never noticed this before. I went away determined never to come back, I thought, but the coming back is not what one believes, nor death, nor the importance. Now my thoughts have by chance turned toward Algeria, due to this terrible paper accident and here they are: the Dog and the Bike, intact, dead more alive than ever before. Forever in the place of life and death.

One cannot imagine the Clos-Salembier without them, I think, I was expecting my brother, he would appear at the end of the same drive, yesterday is here I thought, all that's missing is the chain and padlock on the gate, we lived under their signs: the chain and the lock, the Dog and the Bike, imprisonment and flight, I turned toward the armchair—brother on my right, in a little while my brother would be there, was there, therefore is there, all I need is to say Bike for there to be Dog, Clos for Salembier, to say grace for grace and vice versa, just as the Dog had incarnated disgrace so the Bike played the role of grace, on the one side my father on the other my mother-with-Omi, all around us the besiegers, otherwise known within that room as the kidzarabs or just zarabs, as you like.

Both had been actors in fate's mockery, what was given was taken back, I noted, I shall tell my brother that, what was refused was granted in the end. The author of the Clos-Salembier, I shall say to my brother for it seems to me today that we were in a book without knowing it, the author kept his artistic or theatrical eye on things, each event and each person always had his shadow and his light, the one always had the other as other, to each his own internal opposite, grace in disgrace, disgrace in grace, the one going on ahead of the other which repeats it and displaces it onto the Dog the Bike, my brother and me one of us beyond or outside the other. And in the book of the errors and trials of which the two of us alike, and we alone, are the guardians, it is the destiny of the Dog that to my mind is the metaphor at the heart of the whole story, the family's *transfigure* and the epitome of our Algerias but for my brother it's the Bike. Or so I believed. I was expecting him to appear on a bike, I mean, getting off his soulless bike, framed in the gate and there he is. There's my brother I say and There He Is. There is the Dog my brother denied, the most wretched of the gods and most divine among the wretched who shrieked and howled yapped in the Algerian amphitheater swept by violent blue winds.

I recognize you, Fips, I say, you are one, you are unforgettable. At this very moment he jumps through the frail odorous mist stretched taut between our now and our yesterday, a fresh wound, more as if tossed than galloping, straining as he always did to clear the fences between him and the just life. Eyes popping. With the soul's effort to claw free of prisons. Furious, for he is the Fury in the Erinye family, sacred Anger, that's him. Wild Beast was his name when my father loved him. A small dog no bigger than my cat in which he returns. But immense. I have his soul in my skull, I have his teeth and his rage painted on my feet and hands, I have the Dog, the Whole Dog, from the origins to what came next, engraved in the membrane of my memory. I have the Dog as Master and abandon as guide as vital being as mortal being and as betrayed being. My soul the Dog. My wild transfigure.

We who had always waited in vain for a third child, we were beyond ourselves with excitement when our father announced the substitute: thus we were to have a baby, a child by our dying father. Right away we started building the nest. We fixed up the shoe box. The whole garden lent a hand, dry bougainvillea leaves, chicken fluff, squatting in front of the box we brooded over the dog idea on earth as in heaven. The arrival smaller than a rat but just as brown and just as fidgety. The child our father gives us is a narrow nervous little yellow dog with a gentle catlike mask. This little ratter went after the garden rats, a terror for fat and thin alike, and with a great bound he cleared the spikes of the high gate and then without turning or slowing down soars over the whole neighborhood right to the end of the trolleybus line. We who wanted to incarcerate him in our tenderness. He won't be laid to sleep in the cradle. We struggle. We put him to bed, we pull the sheet up over him, we want a child, we push him down, he won't stay put, up he bounces like a cork we must reconsider our presumptuous ways. This twinge of loss of the made-to-order object we never had. There is no consolation. We are very small, our feelings disproportionately huge. We feel ourselves less lovely. The Dog is outside, he doesn't fit in our box. We love him from farther off. It is my father who looks after the child. Who puts drops in his eyes. Both of them my father and the dog have those feverish eyes. Both of them straining toward another world.

And right after that our father died. Overnight the pleasant villa becomes the ravaged township, the besieged city, I never slept again I say, I spent all my nights on the lookout, we lived in the house as in a city promised to destruction, *delenda est* we used to say, it was marked for demolition, one day or other it would be seized and razed I thought at night listening to the banging of the tin roof, combat is a thing you inherit, it's a reactivated memory I say, between the kidzarabs, the assailants on the one hand and the three of us, my brother the dog and me, the assailed, there is no cause for war, the hostility is handed down through the ages, during the reign of my father it slept, with him gone it has reawakened, up it rises just as it lay down, shaggy, unbridled, a sore spot enlarged by centuries of somnolence it is a state independent of the combatants says my brother, a preexistent hate, one grabs everything one can lay a hand on and one flings it, it is the projectility instinct, it is an Algerian phenomenon says my brother, it was raining. We take shelter under the enormous wooden shields, under a hail of stones, remember the attacks on the house says my brother, remember the munitions, I say, beside the armchairs upended to form a palisade we line up our cannonballs, lumps of Algerian clay baked by the sun, which smash into red dust when they hit the target, I can remember a horrible story says my brother, two young Arabs who were fighting in front of the house, one got on top, he picks up a stone as big as a fist and he started pounding the head of the one underneath as hard as he could, howling in his face to the very last says my brother, he mashes his face howling big sobs look says my brother look says my brother howling to the very last, but still we mustn't exaggerate, says my brother, on my bike when I was part of the swarm of bikes coasting down to the bottom of the hill all the way to Lyon Street, there was never any problem, but around the house instead of my dead father, Hostility had risen from its lethargy, right away it emerges from under the ground and the hunt that throws everything off, that embroils, that insults, the hunt is after us.

We fought back. But the Dog is taken hostage. We don't allow him to fight, that would be a massacre. We tie him up, consign him to his cage. Rain splatters the bars. The Dog is beaten. We don't let him defend himself. The Dog stops sleeping. Skin stretched taut, hair matted frothing at the mouth black foam in his eyes, he runs around howling at the wire of his cage or clawing up the red roses in a hail of shot.

What wounds our spirit is nothing. For the Dog the calamity is double. He suffers our fate and his own to boot. We are shut in, whereupon we shut him in. He suffers the double misfortune of being us and of not being us. We lock up our own brother, for the Dog it is hell, we ourselves clamp our father's heir in irons, there is no more law, the world is topsy-turvy and the Dog has been betrayed. I ought to have spoken to him, I say. To the dog? asks my brother. Am I Jewish, the Dog wondered I say, that I don't believe says my brother. But what does Jewish mean wondered the Dog, and Arab, and dog, friend, brother, enemy, Papa, liberty nothing exists save injustice and brutality. *Here I am, alone on the earth, having no more brother, sister, no father nearby, no friend only my solitude for company. The most sociable and loving of beings is unanimously outlawed. I am caged as in a dream and I don't sleep anymore. And I, detached from them and tied to a strand of wire, what am I?* And I, I thought, I never shone any light on his darkness. After the attacks I avoided going by the cage where he continued howling long after the shooting stopped. I fled his fearful face. I only thought about fleeing this country of chained-up creatures, that chain of chainings-up, the unleashing of the chained-up who in their turn start chaining. As soon as my father died this memory of him began to die as well. I can still see my father with his memory my little wild fever-struck brother.

One doesn't get over the Clos-Salembier, I say, one lives for a few years in the Clos-Salembier and one is marked for life, I say, but really I thought that one day had sufficed to mark me for life, in a single day one razes a city, one is covered with scars in a night, for the whole of one's life I say, then for a lifetime when one wants to dream the horror, the execution of the idea of being human, the abandon of all hope of justice, one dreams of the

Clos-Salembier with the Dog, you are exaggerating says my brother, but that's exactly what I mean: the Clos-Salembier was the Algerian exaggeration and the Dog was my tragedy. The Dog was the innocent one, the prisoner, the only one of us to be reduced to total impotence, deprived of the right of reply, deported, handed over to the madness of the times. I didn't speak to him. I don't tell him that injustice, hate, cruelty had all the rights, that they hunted down and devoured the innocent, they break bones and souls without end, right up to the day when, who knows why, they fall as suddenly as the wind, and if one is still alive one can see another world rise, in which a warm breeze blows and one shares one's bread and meat with the Dog. In the Clos-Salembier, I saw no end, no bread, no peace, I didn't know, I didn't believe, my heart howled in my cage. The Dog like me. I told myself if ever it opens I'll flee, I knew neither courage nor hope. And the Dog like me, no bread, no peace, no hope. Hate and absurdity. All of us were mad dogs, each against the other but we were dogs left free. The Dog, the Dog alone, prisoner. What's more he had ticks. Madness is catching. We turned mean, we bit each other, my brother and I, both of us, we bit each other and ourselves. Between attacks, I would read. I climbed into a book, I sat down on the branch farthest from the ground, I plunged into the leaves of a book, I flew away.

What is unspeakable about Fips's fate is that he constituted himself prisoner, a captive of the repugnant stratagem that Omi-with-Mummy, we two going along, had invented: we let the Dog out only once a day, before giving him his bowl of food, which for the same reason we filled once a day, and the Dog was in on the plot. The minute the door of the doghouse opened out he sprang into the universe and famine brought him back to his chains.

I will depart, I will leave all of Algeria Clos-Salembier behind me, I will never come back, even in my imagination, everything that surrounds me here, I used to think as I read, in the exaltation of reading, will vanish for ever, I will never suffer again, I will never hurt for the blind, the Arabs, the cripples, there will be no trace of the dog, nor of the high school, nor of the trolleybus, nor of the shantytowns, everything will be erased, blown away, annihilated, I would think, but from time to time I thought the contrary, and sometimes I would love what I hated in spite of myself in spite of everything.

I was reading. Someone rings. I am reading. Someone rings at the chained and padlocked gate. I order my brother to go and open it. Half-dozing

I emerge from my book, furious, and I stamp my foot on the ground outside the kitchen. This is where the dark night of misunderstanding springs up. Here, in a gush, comes the Dog. I didn't see it coming. I didn't see the Dog curled up in front of his kennel, still haggard-looking after an assault, see me land on one foot in front of his nose. He thought I was attacking. It seemed monstrous to him that now I, even I, should attack him. No crime or betrayal is foreign to one's own family he thinks. And with a great raucous shudder he pounces on the foot that I aim at him. I shall die of this bite, for it doesn't let go of me it digs in and in, penetrating right to my heart, this is where we enter folly's eternity, I thought, my head in a swirl of scarlet clouds. The teeth went on. We had grown inseparable. We no longer budged, harnessed to pain. The Earth toppled to one side.

Aïcha pulls a sheet from the washtub boiling in the yard, she twists it into a damp rope and she brings it down on the back of the Dog ten times. At the thirteenth blow the Dog rolls over on his side. Our feet torn Aïcha and I shout and cry, and cry and shout. The supernatural Dog. The sky extremely blue. The wounds like grating laughter in our life. Broken halt delirious we exit from the scene on all fours each of us beaten and vanquished for the time of all times.

In the days that followed he and I experienced the lowest form of family life: resentment under the same roof, a poisoned silence. The poison is not the hate, it's the ebbing of love. The days between us are separate rooms. We are joined in avoidance.

Ticks as fat as chickpeas were devouring him, says my brother. That made him a kind of saint.

Fearfully we extracted the monsters my brother and I. The Dog's suffering makes me sorry for myself, I do not love lepers as myself, between us seethes an absence of reconciliation. The Dog gets me on my wrong side, I don't leap into the flames to save him.

Job was the Dog, only I understood that too late the way one understood Job, too late and in part. He is plagued, god was well hidden, the father who was mother is dead, and now the pestilences and sores. They devour him whole, these proofs of the devil's existence, which don't care that dogs don't have hands. Fips feels his life draining into their stomach and without a hope of doing battle. Every day, teeth yanked out puffy with a bloody mush. A nightmarish demography, they come up out of everything and nowhere, colonizing the vampirized body in a slow-motion frenzy. I myself was among their victims.

I feared having his death on my head. An obscene fear of seeing the one I didn't love enough die, since I would not give my life for him I can no longer share in his death, I cross the garden bounding over the flames, the way the Dog used to bound when he still hoped to reach the shore of life one day. When at last the remains of the Dog departed mourned by my brother I wasn't there. I had got out of Algeria just in time I tell myself just before the expiry date.

Nobody remembers his death. He lived to be very old, says my brother. He was eight I say. The five mouths stitched to my feet.

And yet I thought now I loved him, but no more than myself over there in the garden of war, I didn't love myself and I fought myself, and yet I loved Fips, I feel that still, but not in the Clos-Salembier, I loved him later on.

I used to read in the Clos-Salembier because it was impossible to survive without books, I mean to live without light, without mind or spirit, without reality without sleep without peace without bread since everything that occurred in front and in back of the chained gate was shouts folly stupidity darkness slinging stones and pitching earth. Therefore I got from one day to the next from one book to the next without books I'd have been sunk, and which books who cared, it sufficed that there be a foot-sized rectangular volume on which to cross the abyss, donkey, airplane, eagle, cart anything will do I slip from one back to the next I think from Pascal's thoughts to the thoughts of the Comtesse de Segur, and my brother meanwhile does the abyss on a bike. Book and Bike transport us equally, all we ask is to be released, sometimes my brother reads Spirou the way I read *The Idiot* it's all hay for the donkey bones for the Dog, sometimes I read Hercule Poirot the way my brother reads the second volume of *Crime and Punishment* the volume Crime was never there, all our books are hand-me-downs, my brother reads Punishment, we are destined to know Punishment before having known the Crime, the author of our book has a philosophy: first the Punishment, then the Crime. Or maybe it's that one of us is the Crime the other the Punishment, in which case, without a doubt, I am Crime.

Everything was big and strong, I mused, thinking of the violence that inspired us, I read the way he pedals the way I read we pedaled with all our strength, swept away by dangerous descents.

—I don't get the fragrance of the Algerian soil in this book, says my brother.

—Exactly what I don't want I say, no earth smell. I want the shit smell of the human excrement dropped at the foot of the trees in the Arcades Wood, sentinels, our father called them.

—Whatever you say my dear, says my brother.

I'm making a dash for the end of this chapter now, what with the Bike and the Two-Wheeler it's time to get out of the Clos-Salembier cage and come up to the present.

—Doyouremember says my brother and I say doyouremember then my brother says doyouremember and then I in turn say doyouremember, whereupon my brother says doyouremember, then I say doyouremember, all it takes is for one of us to say doyouremember and then the other doyouremembers right back bright and early in the morning, whereupon walking fast and barefoot on the boiling asphalt, we take the untarred alleyway on the other side of the vacant lot, down past Madame Bals the grocery lady brandishing her ladle, foul-mouthed, and without stopping in the sun and occasionally in the shade barefoot and doyouremembering one another we arrive at Arcades Wood, which we cross quickly without meeting another human being just the two of us between the pine tree parasols. Heat sizzles on the needly roof. The going down unthinkable except together on our four bare feet with the satiny red dust between our toes forgotten at last by the brutality of the times. We cut across the empty museum, a somber unlikelihood whose construction we doyouremember a silent sign that we are cutting through the same dream. At which point we exit the cradle of the dream in black and white and arrive at the blue municipal pool violently blue icy glacially blue into which we let ourselves drop like two incandescent stones. We come out of the water brand-new. Doyouremember the sandwiches that crowned the two heroes. Here my brother doesn't doyourmember with me. Never mind never mind. I roll over on my left side and snuggle my head into the shoulder of my dream. This is our page of bliss. We were in the *b*'s, in the bath, arbor, bower, umbrellas, blue of sky, it is all so much and endless and yet brief the whole time we walk together briskly from bliss to bliss, from wood to wood, until an idea of death jumps out at us, for the Wood given by my father also came to remind us of his end.

After all says my brother turning toward me it was a good bike. It was heavy. It had three speeds. It suited me. We did all kinds of things together, the two of us. We went into town with the kidzarabs funny there were no problems we hitched rides on the trucks coming back up. You brace the wheel against the curb twenty yards ahead we threw ourselves out like loonies as they went by. It was a crazy swarm of bikes with kids I didn't know all grabbing the same truck chain with the trucks coming in the opposite direction but you never got to do that.

We weren't all on the same chain, my brother corrects himself, if you say truck it has to be credible, technically, you've got *a* truck, you've got *a* chain dangling behind, I took the chain, there was an edge, with *five* or *six* kids hanging on to it, you have to be careful not to let go, the truck drivers honked to scare us off they stuck out their fists to insult us and they didn't stop, looklook says my brother.

My brother and I are seated in the little wicker chairs on the balcony of the house, the pine forest infinite at our knees.

—Nothing here reminds me of Algeria my brother starts up again. As soon as he arrives, we take our places in the armchairs and mysteriously it all starts to start up again. Everything reminds my brother that nothing here reminds him in the least of Algeria. This is how we communicate sitting in the chairs that are not the Clos-Salembier chairs, that are-not-the-chairs that is to say that they are the non-chairs of the Clos-Salembier we can't sit down in them—we two my brother and I—without noticing the point to which these little chairs have nothing in common with *our* chairs, the immense armchairs-of-war, our gigantic armchairs painted a flaky green, our metamorphosing chairs which served us, depending on how we turned them, as boats, destroyers, tanks, inns, as

The sea is not the sea, the sky is nothing like the sky, the pines, when I look at pines from here all I see are husks of pines, nothing but pines reproduced, when you define these pines you must tell the truth, they are stupid pines, look at that pine, it goes straight up look, twenty yards straight up look I tell you it's stupid and after twenty yards a feather duster, looklook says my brother whereas the Algerian pine is a parasol pine, and not stupid, a graceful twisty velvety sunshade, you must tell the whole truth, looklook exclaims my brother, as all the garden pines stiffen at his looklook and take a step toward us, look how ridiculous that pine on the right is, it is grotesque here the stupid pine is grotesque and you don't say it, and I am the only one who feels all that, thinks my brother crushing the infinitesimal armchair—a fly compared with the giant armchairs of war— beneath the weight of his large regretful body, and I can't even tell you that I am the only one who feels this since clearly, thinks my brother, you feel nothing of what I feel, the proof is you are able to *live here* hee-ere. The more I come up here solely to see you the more convinced I am that you did not know Algeria, the more I feel myself objectively in danger of mu- tilation, since you may have totally renounced that which at bottom united us, he thinks

and I, silent and not stirring at his side, I listen with my whole heart to what his mind intones, I can still read him, my brother, by touch, listen- ing to myself listen to him feeling myself feel his great anger coming from the Clos-Salembier to blow on the straight French dummies without ever succeeding in twisting them to fit his old taste, at this very moment I fol- low him, thinking I am alone, you jettisoned that country which then jet- tisoned yourmother and me, all the while thinking again about this not my Algeria, which turns me upside down and inside out and utterly. The idea of missing Algeria never comes to me. Funny: we are lovesick for years we are capable of any kind of madness in the hope without hope of holding someone in our arms, right up to the day when, years later, this person goes out of my head and becomes a part of the past. And yet for eighteen years *I was truly inseparab.* I hung onto the fence, I watched at the gate I waited for the message: *a* face, a door, a smile. In those days passion for that coun- try was what defined me.

—But what does it mean to know—I say—Algeria, sitting beside my brother, tracking his silences. That which doesn't remind reminds, I say and not-to-know Algeria is also to know it. In one way I have heard of Al- geria I say, and I hear of it still today all the time, there are millions of Al- gerias, there are also hundreds of thousands of Cities of Oran, and each City by the hundreds of thousands and hundreds of thousands of ways of hearing about it. In another way I have heard of Algeria, I say, but so little a trickle of water for my desert.

—Where from? asks my brother.

—From the back of the garden from Aïcha especially, for that is the only Algeria that I was ever able to touch rub against touch again handle stroke arch my back against her calf clamp my mouth between her breasts crawl around on her spicy slopes. I snuggle up to Aïcha from her knees I look at her teeth being the whiteness in the red of her mouth. I was right up against her, I say. But I have never been to her house. I counted her, I counted her teeth, her hennaed toes, her children that came out of her afresh each year I recited the names that came out of her Allaoua Baya Zouina Leila Ali faster Allaouabayazouinaleilaaliaïcha.

I have watched her. I watch her sail into the little harbor of the kitchen, borne along slow ample not making a ripple across the invisible water with the heft and lightness of a fishing boat running aground in the sand with a sigh she advances without moving her feet small majesty swaddled till she reaches the backyard. I watch her lower the veil that cradles her rocking a boat among the white boats and underneath it's a woman who is-the-woman and there is no other woman but Aïcha, neither my mother nor Omi being women, my mother is girlish with a touch of boy, Omi is an Osnabrück lady from a distinguished family of photographs, there is no woman among us that's why for my daily woman I wait for the fruit that comes to ripen every morning from the City of Algiers, in our family there is an undercurrent of virility, quite apart from the tiny breasts, walking with short sharp extremely quick steps sober incisive intact of hands not wasting a second between the seconds, use left and right equally, back verystraight not-straight-enough straighten up suck in your tummy except my brother, in *our* house with the accent on *our,* we don't do woman, we do quickly, to compensate. But here comes Aïcha slow creamy a jug of milk about to boil which doesn't boil over stirring the delectable thicknesses from within a jelly delightful to contemplate for its infinitesimal quivering. Comes to me gliding over the bright water a trajectile I unroll from the gate right to the kitchen so as to watch her come round and finish her race no rush no rush the Aïcha that with a firm heart I tug to the shore of the kitchen and French windows of my bedroom reeling in the line.

Everything a woman can be and everything that can be a woman Aïcha is sometimes big sometimes having thrown off the litter and often turning up with her arms full of the previous child in the shape of a small divinity carefully dirty, blonde locks braided with spider webs flies on the eyelids and pearls of snot in the nostrils, the jewels of the city, the shells hanging from Algeria's neck.

What is left of "Aïcha" who died long ago: volumes and volumes. Art. "Algeria" as a name caressing the untouchable. The velvety name of flee-ing. The beauty of the soft, a rare and difficult beauty. The flabby breasts deliberately badly hitched up, which makes each one autonomous. The round eyes wholly brown wet glistening like brown moons outlined in kohl. The flesh pastries, the look of a layer cake which I still find enticing, and it's the way it all fits together that bowls me over, the multiplication of the same parts of the doll for which I would have sold my soul, the endless number of shes of which she is made.

Without her—no point in imagining what is not. I shall not preterize Aïcha. I am conjugated by her. The whole time of the Clos-Salembier I dreamed of going to Aïcha's house one day. The musics at night. They floated up from distant terraces. From someone's roof made of tiles or corrugated tin. And I never went. To her house. Was there a house? We don't know. Aïcha, pronounces my brother. What a story, I say, what mattered for my brother was Aïcha's daughters and for me it was the mother but to my way of thinking Aïcha was the bread the cake the fruit the well the shade the repose canaan the love of the lambs for the mother's udders salvation, a woman of great beauty who knew a few French words all the other words were in her eyes in her hands in her laughter. And the name of our Story of the Clos-Salembier. And to think that we loved her and called her all those years— our Aïcha—who was everything for me and did not know it and me neither I didn't know it to know it, I lived it is all, besides living was my way of thinking and her skin was the book. I loved the feel of the name Aïcha, nothing sentimental, all sensuous and infantile. And in the end her name wasn't Aïcha and just as none of us knows where this name that wasn't her name came from, so none of us knows which of us learned it from whom and how. Now we all know that Aïcha was really called Messaouda. But too late. Something is done, we do not exactly know, as usual, whether it is the harm that is done, whether what is done is the harm, as I thought when I first heard, from my brother probably, this story of Aïcha who is Messaouda, whom all of us including my father always called something else, and that at the time I was horrified, but for the last two or three years I only think that the harm is done. At the time I was appalled: we who were so careful, my brother and I, to keep the family from ever committing an aggression against a person's name the way others always did, we who refused to tolerate the least faux pas around the house, we the flayed, the night watch the moral guardians of the family which upset us dreadfully when at the Clinic we caught my mother calling the cleaning woman Fatma whose real name was Barta, we the two righteous ones up in arms the minute we caught a family member or friend in the corridor saying one of the dirty or dirtying words and names, we who had never failed to fustigate had sinned for ten years and of all people against Aïcha who is Messaouda or the other way round.

—They always said she was an Ouled Naïl my mother recounts. They said she was a dancer—then when she had enough money they said she married an old man. But I never knew how much to believe of what they said, nor whose story it was. It was a story. The only thing I know about Aïcha is that I made a big mistake once delivering her, says my mother, I was a beginner, you don't know where the snag is, the Moors says my mother (a word we guardians ended up tolerating for lack of a better term, but only in its plural form, the Moors, fine, "the" Moor, never, without managing to give my mother a grammar lesson, we outlawed "the Moor") the Moors she says under our stern gaze, would push, it was their custom, she pushes, she pushes, and I didn't stop her says my mother avoiding saying Aïcha, it's crazy, if there's a pillar or rope, they grab it she pushed all night long and I didn't know there was no point. Nothing is more dangerous than doctors and midwives who are not qualified which I was at the time since I was a beginner. Later I understood. Make haste slowly. What yourfather should have done. Slow down the contractions that don't do any good, I should have told him to conserve his strength and jump at the opportunity. As a beginner I made big mistakes that I stopped making later on. But the mistakes that are made can't be unmade. That Aïcha hanging onto a rope on some sort of veranda and whose real name is Messaouda I can't get her out of my mind. It was the last child. I never set eyes on her husband. All the rest is a story. "Ali," I say, the baby god with flies on his eyelids propped up under a chechia.

I wonder where her tomb is. The last page of the life foretold of a woman, solid, knocked up year after year, each year a daughter abandoned forever in an unknown husband, the calf is borne away the cow cries all day the following day or the one after she stops bellowing naturally. Bahia the gentle limper, my father saves her from tuberculosis from which he doesn't save himself. Later Bahia vanishes into a backwoods husband, and of her henceforth one says "it appears." My father cares for the lame heifer, a tough job. Lives of cows and calves. I also sucked on Aïcha's tits. I will do anything to get away from this country, I thought, and no longer ever have to listen to the mother bellow all day long right up to the moment when the bellowing switches off without anyone knowing why, naturally.

—I never knew her husband, all I remember of Aïcha is her oldest son after-the-French he became Director of the Hospital says my mother to finish up Aïcha's story that was the end of him whereas we thought here's a beginning the hospital went to his head and suddenly he became a drinker, it was a disaster they always said he no longer knew his own mother, but he no longer knew himself. And that's all I know about that Aïcha clinging to a rope all night on some sort of veranda, it was crazy says my mother, and she looks askance at the midwife she once was. But it's a good long while she is no longer her. On the couch in my study the elderly girl who is my mother-of-stories, leans a little, very upright, over the pages of the medical text.

—Were you ever in Aïcha's house? I hoped.

—No says the midwife. I only went for deliveries this one went on all night, never shall I forget that pillar which was in the house obviously.

Heart pounding I don't give up even today I keep watch perhaps a door will open in the City of Algiers if I rap hard enough at my mother's memory even now I skirt the wall, I run my fingers over it and I dream of entering into the country of which I am the stubborn abortion.

—Invited? I ask.

—Invited? No!

She responds without hesitation. With evident astonishment. She bats the word invited back at me. It seems utterly incongruous to her. Another of your dreamed-up notions she makes me feel. A word completely out of place, a reality, in other words, with no reality.

We are seated on the couch in my study. It's a police station, this couch. I ask her questions and she replies. The Algiers police inspector was very nice and as inspector truly exasperated by "those Arab stories," my mother goes on, "Arab stories" were unlikely tales. People went to him bearing a mishmash of tales, he was fed up with them, he called me in, he told me Madame Cixous another of those "Arab stories," I'm fed up with them! A pair of panties full of blood, I'm fed up says the inspector, what next, coming from the Clinic, it's about a husband, a woman, a taxi driver, a delivery where all went well, I've asked you to come down for the panties, I have to, what has she come to the station for, the husband wants to know why this blood, these panties, *before* they wouldn't have dared to go to see the inspector with the panties full of blood but they must learn that the inspector is not to be pushed around, *before* they wouldn't even dare go to see the judge for such nonsense, but now they dare to bring a pair of panties into the police station as an Arab complaint please sign here and spare me these Algerian stories there's the difference says my mother, *before* they didn't dare *after* you could add the judge the inspector to the cast and for the final scene bring in the prison director. *Before* there's no courtroom no courthouse there's only the family and the Clinic *after* you've got the police station on the left and therefore the tragedy which is sometimes comic sometimes terrifying. Each time that I am *invited* to go down to the station, I wonder is it a tragedy, is it a comedy, in case of risk I go out veiled, so as to slip past the concierge character. I'm going to stop there, says my mother confusedly, she stops, on her face perplexity she is wondering, I thought, why all of a sudden she has swept us off to the Algiers police station in my study. She is embarrassed. She is feeling that places which have nothing to do with one another have become communicable in the most improbable fashion. I could enlighten her, but I haven't time. I don't want to lose the scent. I let her take a sip or two of café au lait. Then I return to my interrogation. Once again I say the incongruous word. I did say *invited*. I don't say one thing when I mean something else. A country in which one is never invited can you call it a country, where one lives for decades can you call it a country where one has children, where one has a job, one is not invited, one is not in trade, one is not a mechanic, one is the midwife for the people of the country, if it is a country, a country without a door without a threshold is like an infant born without an ear perhaps things are wrong inside too but maybe things are not so simple in this affair.

On the one hand you have the midwife, but also the German, irreversible in my opinion, and above and beyond the German there's the Frenchwoman, which to my way of thinking my mother is not in the slightest but according to the official papers and the language she is, above and beyond the German who is French there is the Jew that in my opinion she is absolutely not from the Jewish point of view she has no religion or tradition she doesn't go to the synagogue ever, she declares having been something of a loner, in Oran you had your family as world, add to that the German refugees you met on the benches of Little Vichy and the Promenade de l'Etang, the Hellmanns, the Fülds, the Hagenauers, the Morgensterns, the Flörsheims, in Oran there was the family on one hand, Germany cut and boned on the other, blood-tinged Germany, benches full of Germans cast up on the shores of Oran, gasping, all these people exiled and deported some of them in Germany some in the south of France, others in Algeria behind French barbed wire, some with tattoos others without, they all met up on the benches, one bench in a public park means two Germans, as family breadwinner "nurse" standing in for the doctor, she declares she didn't have time to get to know Algeria, but she'd heard of it, she was a little wary of the French, first in Oran-under-Vichy, later from 1946 on in Algiers she never tried to socialize with them and vice versa, where we lived there weren't many opportunities, she says, in yourfather's day—1946–1947—a group of us were Jews but from 1948 on she had no illusions, doors closed, except those of the synagogue through which one must pass if one wishes to enter the

Jewish milieu as a Jew. But she doesn't even know where the synagogue was in Algiers, in Oran we used to pass in front of it but we didn't go to the synagogue even for the holidays not Omi nor Granny nor yourfather's sisters, I might perhaps have enjoyed being part of a group of people where they celebrated the holidays, she says, but you can't have the holidays without the synagogue and neither she nor Omi were ever pillars of the synagogue in either Osnabrück or Oran; not your father either he was veryJewish beginning with Vichy in the sense of being antivichy and not liking the synagogue. I got along fine without religion, she says. In Osnabrück unfortunately there was a rabbi who used to give us Hebrew lessons, unfortunately he wasn't very nice, he was proud and a pig Dr. Krakauer he rather put us off the women sent him packing furthermore there were condoms on the ground in the courtyard of the synagogue he had a very beautiful wife but who had tuberculosis fortunately she died very quickly. Nonetheless, she must emphasize, there are fatherly rabbis. She never knew one, but she imagines they exist. She wishes to add this: there was a handsome intelligent noble rabbi everybody adored him and admired him, all of Germany was talking about him. But I didn't know him, she says. He must have been from a big city, perhaps he was from Düsseldorf. Afterward he left for the United States. There was therefore *one* handsome rabbi. The fact that she didn't know him doesn't mean he didn't exist she points out. The fact that she has never heard of a handsome and intelligent rabbi in Algeria doesn't mean anything either.

Another "Jewishstory" says my mother, and not to be repeated in front of strangers she says.

Besides she doesn't have the feeling of belonging to a community she had never heard of before arriving in Algeria and if her father-in-law hadn't died shortly before she arrived she probably wouldn't have married my father who could not so easily have opposed his father's refusal to let him marry an Ashkenazi who had never heard the word Sephardi before coming to Oran. In the midst of all these complications which have in common some questions about doors, entries, admissibility, there is my mother, this is the important thing, a woman if she's a woman, who I can imagine I thought is very likely difficult to admit for an interesting reason: she has a lack of complication that is tantamount to a complication so sophisticated others can hardly conceive of it. Whatever smoothes things over she has not, whatever provides vital lubrication for social relations, she never avails herself of. A lack of ruse, lack of duplicity, therefore a lack of politeness, lack of lipstick, lack of detours, a brutal uprightness is a cowlick on the mind, an unbearable simplicity of manner and thought, to the point of an absence of meanders and depths, no internal distance. In a country where for some the veil has become an organ, a retina, where for others outright cunning, avowed hypocrisy, are idiomatic, where everybody pays lip service to the contract, my mother is an absurdity an irregularity and an offense. Honesty is a criticism of dishonesty, she doesn't want to know about it. She doesn't realize. She is one of a kind. She doesn't know she is an exception. And what might save her, sentimentality, she calls toadying, and toadying she calls: corruption. A midwife she has just hired brings her croissants for breakfast? For my mother the case is closed. I am not corruptible says my mother, I will not eat these croissants.

I can see many reasons for not inviting my mother in this country whose conventions she doesn't respect. But the midwife? The celebration, the brand-new baby fresh from the Clinic, the deliveries in the Casbah in Wild Woman Ravine and in the Bouzareah housing projects where she is out wandering around after midnight in the unlit darkness of the besieged city?—There was a curfew, how was I supposed to get home? I get in my car I go round in circles at one in the morning I find my way. Suddenly, in the middle of the road, in the headlights, a box, my last hour has come, a box of explosives, alone at the wheel of the 4 CV without a good-bye to the sky steely stars without a backwards glance, I drive over it. Nothing happened. I drove on. Far behind the newborn is enjoying its first meal. The modesty of one's final hours. Without the so soft Franciscan feathery garb. Modesty of modesties. Modesty up to and including annihilation. So I repeat my question: she mustn't have understood what I was asking her.

—Invited, I say, thinking of the countless invitations the word invited conjures up, invitation, *invitus invitam* with its fabulous accursed, subtle, contrary resources, *dimisit,* its Latinate shimmers, its twists, its secrets, its jealousies, its hearts, some good and sugary, others honeyed, others bitter and lying,

invited as in invited, I say, weren't you? like in a house, in a tent, around a fire, as in kindly requested, expected, authorized, received, urged, accepted—normal I say. Never? Think. I invite you.

She thinks. Invited, no. She thinks. She leafs through her diary. She runs up and down the hallways. The arcades, flights of stairs, streets, back alleyways. Once—she comes up with—once I was invited to a marriage. That's the story about the Algerian midwife who told her gigolo to invite me to dance all the time with the idea of getting rid of him. It was of no interest to me. This time I was in someone's home. She had huge mother-of-pearl-encrusted armoires, says my mother, delighted to have found an invitation.

Drawers stocked with the jewelry of corruption. She tells me if ever the police are after me I'll throw on a veil and have myself exported to Morocco. One day I heard from the prison Director a very nice man whose wife I had delivered that she was there. You know your girlfriend is among us he tells me. She was into prostitution. Another possibility. I am astonished says my mother that she didn't have time to put on her veil. The young man got married in the end. A few years later his wife delivered a baby at my place. A fine boy, in 1971 just before the end of the Clinic that nobody suspected was destined to go down lock, stock, and barrel in February of that year.

But otherwise no. I was never invited no, says my mother at peace now. And she closes the empty album of invitations.

—Why? I say and I wished I hadn't. My mother says: people didn't invite midwives!

That's one explanation.

—To Arab homes? I don't think so says my brother.

And yet I hope.

—I had a friend at Bugeaud says my brother. They were few and far between at the lycée. Your normal involuntary separation a state you are born in a place where the houses don't open. You don't know that things can be different. On the one hand the people go to eat their Mouna at the Palestra. They believe it's Eternity including me says my brother.

—On the way to the mountain we went by the marabout I say.

—We lived side by side says my brother involuntarily and vice versa.

I knew Algeria in the flesh dive into the warm water at Tipaza stroll dreaming under the mastic trees and among the ruins my brother daydreams, I always had the feeling of getting out much more than you did, says my brother.

—I wanted to go in, I was going to say, but he was off again on the Bike in the opposite direction, into Aïcha's sensual house I say.

The legless cripples on their skateboards. You also see them in front of the post office and in Government Square. At the Clos-Salembier the kids zoom off on the crippled skateboards nimble they race down Laurent-Pichat Boulevard despite the trucks. An unlucky kid ends up legless on his own board.

The blind eyeless from purulent meltdown of the syphilitic eye and blinded by the purulence of the mind's eye, mental cripples, men without noses and French without a sense of smell, lepers with their cankered French consciences and Arabs shipwrecked in their beings, rusty cans, bowel movements in the staircases and in the midst of all that some places are sheer paradise.

—In Germany I didn't suffer either says my mother who returns willingly in her thoughts to Osnabrück but not in reality, who goes from Osnabrück to Algiers with a stopover in Oran naturally, having never been less at ease in one city than in another, nor more settled down either, never a little more or a little less in one of the cities that she loves to explore, especially when she finds herself at the wheel of a shopping cart, romantically astray in one neighborhood or other, death crouched under a box, all alone in her shell on wheels, and if at that point the wind the darkness the drenched road the stars dumping their buckets of water on top of the feeling of rubberized impermeability, I can feel life says my mother enchanted, she glides on ahead of me, and what does all that mean: nothing else. The *gesunder Antisemitismus,* we were used to it, it didn't bother us. The accepted Jews, the doctors the professors, the Jews accepted it. We didn't suffer at school. *One* time I was invited to a birthday party and I went. In summer we went to Norderney, all the Jews went to Norderney, on the North Sea. On the Baltic there were beaches where all the Jews didn't go, in Helgoland there weren't any but at Norderney there were lots—nothing but Jews? I asked—everybody says my mother, I never went to Jewish homes says my mother I was still very German next people began to be Zionist which I never was, every time there is some kind of nationalism I don't go, I have always been international. When we left Germany, I always said "back home" "over here," I said: "the French have no bathrooms, people trim their nails in the metro the secretary only works when the boss is looking." I've got over that. "Back home" is a thing I got over when I arrived in Oran.

But every City has its castes. That didn't bother me. I was too busy with my deliveries. As a midwife I was always international. The baby is an international newborn. The Clinic had two doors that were always open.

That's another explanation, I thought. My mother isn't bothered, she doesn't realize, everybody else is bothered, whereupon she is not bothered which never fails to rub people the wrong way, add to that her undisputed reputation for competence, which is not without its value in the medical world, for the doctor it is often a source of irritation but all in all he'd just as soon pass the buck to the competent midwife as to the incompetent one.

But for many people who come to consult her my mother is a moral danger because with her you never know where the moral danger lies, outside the realm of deliveries it's unclear, she excels at delivering, but it isn't only the births that count, in addition there are all the stories, particularly the "Arab stories." But you never know where she stands in these stories, in theory she is "French" in reality she's anything but "French" for the patients, for whom the concept "international" has neither meaning nor currency. Somebody you cannot simply hate as it is normal everyday and just for patients to hate the French, you cannot love either. A brief expanse of foreignness. To what point, in what essential, natural, innate manner passes description. My brother and I are ourselves bothered by it we ourselves cannot get accustomed. With her, the patients feel, I thought, and I took the word *feel* rather than the word *think* because this thing that has always made her the uninvited guest, and us uninvited by association, eludes thought: it is a lack of the sense of hostility cheek by jowl with its opposite. On the one hand my mother is utterly oblivious to ranting filthy insults, racist abuse, anti-Arab or anything else, my mother signifies the very impossibility of upbraiding, explosion, aggression, expression of hate, she calls in absent at any scene of violence, deadly and murderous stupidity doesn't come naturally to her, she is immune, never under her roof has she sheltered the idiotic and contagious folly that spreads over the whole City where not a day goes by without hundreds of confrontations big and small, there is even Miss Sharpshooter the Algerian midwife who insults her patients in labor in French she calls them filthy Arabs and that's what things have come to in the City of Algiers people can no longer refrain from vomiting and spitting, even on themselves, even on themselves, it's chronic, a morbid habit, a pulmonary fashion, a tongue, a nervous cough, everybody catches it incubates it in their organism transmits it, all in all it's a state of passion, that's the only explanation for the success of this exalting of the mental nerves, this use of dreadful words, the compulsive expectoration of repulsive words including glory, glair, the glorification of the worst in oneself, the cultural self-congratulation for the verbal glair emitted by the body of society grown undifferentiated in its excesses, this culture, this innate eroticism, they my mother and the midwife are immune to it. Osnabrück's rubberized raincoat has become my mother's skin. There's something wrong. This insensitivity, this stability, is troubling. Nothing touches her internally. The code is missing. For one thing she does not wear the blows one would expect. For another, is she a friend? An ally? Of hate and therefore love, she knows nothing, and thus everyone except for me could hate her, except for me who knows she doesn't know. One day a woman who is not young, a Kabyle woman who has *made arrangements* with an unmarried mother comes to see her with the abandoned child, poor boy, two years old and without a birth certificate, make me a certificate that says I gave birth to him here and the child will have a mother. So what does my mother say? "You are out of your mind Madame, you are over sixty, who will believe the child is yours?"—says my mother another unlikely story. She utters these commonsense words to this woman of over sixty who has come from the Kabyle to become the arranged mother of a two-year-old child still with neither birth nor luck. It is unbelievable, I thought, my mother is crazy, we always knew it, she is in the right where society is left and wrong. She refuses to draw up certificates for women who have not given birth in the Clinic, and she calls those papers forged, in a world where apart from the forged there is no luck and no truth. She is not crafty like everyone else. She does not give the answer, she is a false door, she opens and behind the door another door is closed, she never sends anyone away ever, people send themselves away when they come in contact with her. My mother forever virginal, untouched, me printed once and for all, I grasp the evil I see, I've got Algeria in my lungs in my throat I don't find it strange that it should turn me hot and cold and bruise my nervous system with its toxic overflow. I attribute the scars of my marked body to the malgerian force of my imagination, but it's not that I think I see what I don't see, it's that I think what I see and I see what the French do not see.

My fat cook says my mother was old, she was a good cook she was good at making a bit on the side. I ordered steaks from the Mozabite. The Mozabites are honest folk. I had ordered twelve of them. She tells me there are only eleven. The Mozabite kept one. I say: let's count. That did the trick. Two of them are clamped together. Here's what she does. She always has her two daughters turn up at noon to eat with her four small children. One day Kheira tells me: she just went to the cupboard. Surreptitiously to the cupboard I go, I open, I touch. There's something hot in there. That's when she darts out of the kitchen. The dart is my cook, with whom I've been fed up for years. What are you doing there? she roars. I say that's what I'd like to know. She is pilfering a bit of couscous, a trifle. I say a bit of couscous you can ask. She bellows there's no de Gaulle anymore to push us around. I quit. I say don't let me keep you. I was delighted but the following day she's back she says I'm back. But you quit. She goes to the labor conciliation board. The judge tells me give her one more chance. I say no I never fired anyone she left all by herself, says my mother.

I say: where is the justice in all that?

I feel an irrepressible shame.

I think: if I was an old cook. I think: if I had an old cook.

I note: I am on the outside of my house, I am nostalgic for what will never exist, there is no judgment, I am outside all the us's, all the us's go by like tanks crushing earthworms with their treads. If I survive, I shall tell all—to no one.

I think: the good cook, the good midwife. Life eats its own hands. The Age of the Mozabite in the desert. I am sad forever. I quit. Nobody stops me.

I oughtn't to have knocked at the door, I thought, the more one knocks the more one feels one is hitting someone then accusing them, about which one feels guilty, one insists, the blows turn around, one begins to speculate one is struck by all sorts of suspect and suspicious thoughts, which doesn't force the door to open on the contrary it gathers in importance and hostility, it was a door it becomes a face, forehead, ulterior motive, another inch and she is going to blab, what she is going to say I am all too afraid of, therefore I will not add to the error of having harassed her with the error by putting absolutely humiliating words in her mouth.

How far one can go with the blows one administers oneself with respect to a closed door is something I experienced almost every week in the Clos-Salembier. At the Clos-Salembier gate. One sees all. We look through the bars. It is an open-closed gate. Forehead against the bars. Our forehead. The forehead. I feel a shameful sadness, sad at being ashamed of being sad: I gave a piece of bread through the bars to a little girl I didn't dare look at on the other side, no I gave nothing, some bread passed from one side to the other, stolen bread, the minute I believe I am giving a piece of bread, I feel it is stolen goods, it is stolen, I steal, I return the stolen goods, I avow I own up; there is no gift hence no bread. A ransom, that's all that passes from one hand to the other hand.

I feel a rage of shame at the gate. I yank off tufts of thyme eyes averted I push the thyme through the gate, so not to see myself not giving holding out the thyme in the hand held out to take the thyme.

Of course I would have stolen I was thinking from the other side. Another reason to get out of this country. I would have robbed myself of course I was thinking.

At the gate we hear Yadibonformage coming we hear his call from afar chiming like a cock crow it's Yadibonformage the cheese man! we shout, the peddler is at the gate. He enters the garden, takes two steps, sets down his basket, squats, he is a thin precise little man Yadibonformage his face reserved serious under his chechia he lifts off the tea towel exposing the basket there is good cheese, he names each object yadlavachkiri, yadizoeufs, yadilinestlé the goods designated and celebrated, cheese, milk, eggs that one lifts one by one and rotates in the sun as if they were the apples of the hens' eyes, from afar, from the steps of the veranda, Omi buys a few eggs half a box of cheese we run from the veranda to the basket, the ceremony's officiants.

At the gate. There is poor Yadibonformage. Today I am alone. Yadibonformage still insists on showing me his goods out of politeness I don't dare turn him away out of politeness. I feel a shy embarrassment. I insist so that he understands I am alone, there is no money. Yadibonformage lifts up the tea towel. I crouch uselessly beside the basket. Yadibonformage shows me the eggs one by one. He asks me if there is any blood. I didn't understand. Which blood? He points to my sex, he asks if there is any blood. A slight astonishment. I say no. I wonder if I said the right thing. Yadibonformage offers me blood. He shows me how. He rubs his forefinger on the edge of the basket. At home that's how they do it. The blood comes. He offers me some. I say no thank you. I am a little unsure about Yadibonformage's proposition. I fear I have a fear regarding the peddler. I get up. I go away. Yadibonformage puts the tea towel back on the eggs. He goes away. I go back into the empty house. I feel as if there's a smirch on my mind. That finger on the basket suddenly it seems to me that I went by a dead cat, I walked in it. I don't exactly know what I must wash how, it is a small dread, a small repugnancy, small indecisive things, bizarre little eggs. Because I don't believe the blood happens like that. The following week he comes back. My brother runs to the gate. Those were black market days.

On the far side of the Clos-Salembier, to the north, on top of the hill next to the church, Françoise's house, straight hard as an equestrian statue its back to the town. Petrified on its narrow base just when it was taking a step toward the church. Not a tree to carve its shadow into the white monument. All around is white, the chalky ground whereas around our house everything is red. Such is the power of France I thought astonished.

I have never been to my friend Françoise's house is what I think every morning at seven thirty at the end of the trolleybus line that takes us to the Lycée Fromentin, which ceases to be the K line when the two of us leap aboard, and becomes our coach but when I take it without Françoise, jumping on at the last second as it is pulling out and even though Françoise is not there still I jump aboard my soul dimmed by regret sorrow and the promise of a storm of pent-up anger. I catch it on the run because the craze of punctuality is stronger in me than the craze of passion, my German side stronger than my French, but if I jump I am torn, half of me simply cannot renounce the need for the lycée the other half cannot walk laughing without Françoise's legs and it is the cut-off top half, my northern head my soldier's helmet that takes the K on the run, in which case it is only this rapidly filling trolleybus, which becomes, as the whistle sounds, a dumpster a truckload a railway car sometimes packed with innocents and a considerable number of women nursing babies, one and all lost in their thoughts and in no way travelers, borne away, daydreaming, submissive ephemera, whose calm is threatening present only at the tips of their buttocks, occasionally big with disorder with shouts of stowaways, with filth, with exposed organs, with pus, with spurts of sperm which seem to me yellowish, with pantomimes of crime, with lofty old men wrapped in patched parchment, faces mummified by very ancient miseries, and hands with sorts of nails inches long, which are crimped and twisted horns like the tireless nails of cadavers. This version of K is the country's hellish revelation, several times a week I catch Hell from the Clos-Salembier to the Main Post Office, with my yearly pass good for two lines, pass! you call out to the conductor, in a voice sure of its rights, a pass for the inferno I announce to myself, and the idea of having a pass reassured me. A season ticket. So it is that I am right at home on the K heads or tails. Just as there are two types of conductors, the gentle ones and the hellish ones. One is all male kindness, the brown milk of compassionate virility, these are the bringers-up of children, cradles, the masculine of breasts. The other with gleaming eyes is devoured by throat-cutting dreams at high noon, women hunts, slit bellies. A few trolleybus images says my brother. Doyouremember. That sort of bastard who would press himself against our buttocks. The fat conductor with a black beard. Eyes gazing into the distance. Doyouremember I say. A few images says my brother. Papa in his light gray suit. He runs up. The trolleybus is moving. He waves. The driver stops, smiling. The same trolleybus a year later the dreamy conductor in his black beard. The K line is our awful secret, mymother-with-Omi have never heard about it, already in the K we guessed at the futility of the tale, never could my mother-with-Omi have done a thing about it, except believe us, we guessed they would donothing out of a wise philosophical resignation acquired in Osnabrück and reinforced in Dresden, he who can change the world is not yet born, says my mother, I am still of the generation where one mends, a seam undone, I take my needle, whereas you you throw it out, a button missing you toss it away, I think that's just life, says my mother, one cannot remake the world they thought, one can only change worlds, says Omi, but I thought only of that. Lacking mybrother to share the idea of suicide, him without me as me without him we would not have managed to keep the idea of suicide at bay, for two must be humiliated together for humiliation to become rage. Those who claim they have never felt the fat conductors rubbing up against their asses, says my brother and that at least once a week should just go to the end of the Clos-Salembier line and take the K trolleybus. Take out *ass* says my brother, take ass out of the book says my brother, but how to do that? So I'm just leaving the girls' asses in I say and I remove my brother's. On the K one would have liked to have no ass.

Which doesn't stop the banana trees the peach trees the medlar trees the palm trees the orange trees the mimosas but the paradise in the middle of which the lone Dog howls does nothing to blur the extraordinary vividness of Hell.

Images. Repeated visions of the truth. All of this stirs my soul to come. Get it down, I thought, on memory's notepads. Describe, I tell myself, when the time comes, if the time comes. If one day the day comes. I shall say: the inside of the world. The reserved howls which fill every place, every square in the City of Algiers. The French who go by with their eyes out, other eyes in the place of seeing eyes. The flight of knives in the dazzling air big birds with a single wing that ends up in a beak. On the walls the signature: "You shall see." But what is written on the walls for all to see is as if it were written on the wall behind the wall. One day I shall recount what went on in the Clos-Salembier. Who will believe me? Who will say the contrary?

Françoise is on time: I take the coach. My South with my North.

She lives in the high white shut-up house that sits on the French tip of the Clos-Salembier where the school the library and the police station gather.

I suggest you call this book Paradise Lost says my brother. You mean Hell Lost I say. Everything we lose is paradisiac says my brother. It's hellish I say. The hell of paradise.

I've never entered the house in the white street sitting veiled at the top of the staircase it peeks through its window-eye. Down below, at the door, I call, I shout the name, how many times, often, nobody answers, I don't get discouraged, I shout because I cannot do otherwise. I want her to come.

The progress we had made the childhood of my brother-and-me compared to the childhood of my mother-and-her-sister it's that if I have never in my life been to my friend Françoise's house, she on the other hand has been to visit me, and several times in the space of a few years I manage to have her, whereas I would go to call her at her door, especially in the morning before the time for the K, for I was always early she always late, I early in the hope, in the urgency of the joy of seeing her come out of her encircled house, of running as fast as our sandals would take us to leap on the K-oach which carries our plot to make the land of Hell into a musical comedy off to school. It was love in friendship the school days of Montaigne and La Boétie, because it was me because it was not him, it had no past and no future and I see my whole life go by between the two stops, my whole life in those days, my whole girl's life takes place between her and me, I feel it is eternal, this is my 1950s eternal life and even today the year 1950 is now. She was three hundred yards from my house, I was two thousand years from hers or vice versa it was possible for her to come to me but for me go to her house was out of the question and the name of this bizarre radical cut between our houses was anti-Semitism. A great anti-Semitic complication making what was possible for me impossible for her. We could meet and inevitably we had to meet since we went to the same school on the same bus and we were in the same class and that was where one began to feel the perverse historical complication, due to an error of my father's when we arrived from Oran I was enrolled in this so-called high school for girls which ever since Vichy avoids Jews, the Jewish girls all went to the other school, Delacroix I believe, but we realized that too late, my father was already dying, and I was in this school to all appearances traditional classic ordinarily anti-Semitic thanks to which my soul was shaped not at all like the soul of my mother who has always been hostile to combativeness whereas I was already shaping up as a combatant on my own in Oran simply from the contact with the poverty of Philippe Street and the Place d'Armes which was good enough for me, but which for my family was a *gesund* poverty a perfectly bearable sort of poverty called "poverty in the sun" and which didn't bother anyone, and now that I was by mistake in the school without Jews, that is to say with a handful of Jewish girls, and without Muslims, that is to say with a handful of Muslim girls, I could obviously not not see what there was to see, those big holes, those blanks or black spots, those gaping rips in the dress in the place of the Jews and the Muslims, making it incumbent upon me to take up a critical space considerably larger than my dreamy inner space. This "health" of the social body I experienced as illness, all those defenses, rejections, doors I turned into a personal malady. In those days I pitted myself daily against the Algerian door personified by Aïcha for one thing, for another against the French door visible in the person of Françoise and her visible house sturdy and of a military whiteness, which I truly did walk by for years and years right up to the last day, and for another against the invisible doors that banged even inside the lycée a sumptuous building in the guise of a School for Girls, a Moorish palace refined in its beauty in which there were no Algerian women, no Moorish women, no palace, since it was a palace-changed, whose occupants, called girls, with their retinue of big and little secretaries, big Head Mistress big and little teachers, every day rehearsed the initial secret program, without being told, hence doubtless with a trouble- and thought-free efficiency: a plan to efface the Algerian being, carried out in the same way as all comparable plans to efface in all the countries which work to enforce total substitution. Substitution, excision, and phantomization, operations carried out with total success insofar as they concern the tools, actors, actresses, operators, workers, consumers, beneficiaries, recipients of the plan. The girl who studies in the lycée believes she is studying in the Lycée she considers her own, bearer of a name as typically French as her own or that of the Clos-Salembier. But I went to the disguised-lycée without believing in it. The first thing I saw when I arrived each morning was that I could no longer discern a trace not a single trace of malgeria, I saw the excised enormity of all I had seen just before I walked through the guarded gate, my passport showing that I belonged to the gate's elect, exorcised, I saw the glaring absence of the country proper which from this side of the border was improper, I saw myself in a palace-tuous place, in a physical and mental disinfection so complete that had I not returned each evening to the purulence of the Clos-Salembier I too would perhaps have metamorphosed into a psychically and mentally excised being. And to think that my father himself enrolled me in mental aberration, where I remained in abeyance, so as not to discard his last letter.

Invisible things brush past me in the inner courtyard, as soon as I am alone I am touched by the ghosts, I am doubled, double, everything is double, all the people who come together and draw apart in the Lycée are double, are doubles, all of them at the same time themselves and a stand-in. The play begins. The film starts to roll. They are all already retrospective. All these people have gone by already. The understudies would one day be replaced. But when? when will the replacement come?

Now I know it will come too late. I know that happiness comes but too late. I know God arrives, too late. In those days in the Lycée I used to think he doesn't come and could think of nothing other than this frozen present. In those days in the Lycée, when I entered and I was inside, I was in an exacerbated outside. On the hooks capes coats jackets I try everything hanging I search for my lab coat my sweater I spend the whole day without managing to dress everything I put on I take off again I wear shoes that are not mine, I am a book of apocalypses written in a language I don't speak and I have no author.

In Oran we were fortunate my brother and I to have entered outside, at the cardboard school, thanks to Vichy we avoided internment in *the plan to efface the Algerian being,* since we ourselves were destined to *the effacement of the Jewish being.* All the big events in Oran that closed their nets around us were sudden expulsions, always without warning and just when we thought we had been admitted thus believed we had got somewhere, a social position, that very place would reject us, first admitted then out again, time's turnstile, first admitted *so as* to be rejected, admitted to the Officers' Club so as to be rejected by the Officers' Club, conscripted into the Army so as to be spit out, enrolled in School so as to be barred from School. It kept us on our toes and gave us meaning. I expected to be chased away, I was waiting for the chase, I was fit for the chase.

Luckily, once this holy outsiderization was stopped by the American landing, it did not stop in our minds or bodies. It continued to make itself felt during the brief years that followed to the point where I never believed in the Lycée Lamoricière, nor in the Lycée Stefan Gsell, under my eyes, under my father's they melted away. I slipped through the walls without any trouble. I thought: next year in Algiers.

I cannot enter Françoise's house where Jews are not allowed but I don't care I've become used to that since Osnabrück, it is strictly forbidden for a Jew to enter this house but it is not totally nor strictly impossible that she make an appearance in the house of the Jew I am used to complexity, such is the tortuous law to which we submit, however she is allowed to come to my house only under certain conditions. On condition there is no contraindication and no obstacle. In addition to our K-oach rendezvous I also absolutely wanted to have her come to my house, tirelessly I filed requests, my friend transmitted them to her parents and sometimes my request was granted, sometimes it was rejected, after a few days. When permission was granted she really came, it only occasionally happened that she was forbidden to go out just at the moment she was about to go out, and that I found difficult to bear, I didn't get into the habit, breathless with hope I remain fixed at the gate, through the bars I can see beyond Laurent-Pichat Boulevard to the spot in the middle of the barbed wire of the vacant lot where she would emerge if nothing kept her. If an obstacle came between my friend and me I was barred from the list of the living in front of the gate the barbed wire of the vacant lot curled around my waist, imperturbable, the bars of the gate escorted me to the door of the tomb. The following week I would file a request. My friend is a marionette, she has all the poignant charms the powers and potentialities, she appears to be coming then it is grace itself touching the earth's red dust suddenly a phone call she is lifted from the ground cracked in two hung disheveled and yanked back behind the curtain in a dark flash. One never saw the puppeteers, authentic arbitrary artists. I know there are two of them and the tale has it that the two people hidden behind the curtain manipulate one another first this one the other one then the other one this one, the mother the aunt, with a wondrous dexterity first the one grants and at the last second the other breaks her word sometimes one refuses and the other refuses even more loudly.

These invisible circumstances, which are unaccountable, since my friend never knows what is going to happen to her what untimely event come from whom inspired by whom prompted by whom, give my friend the heartbreaking charm of the innocent object. She is never to blame for our disgraces and fates she says. Standing at the base of the tower I call up she tells me don't call I call I see the wan eyelid of a curtain slowly blink at the top of the building.

I was awaiting the famous Sunday at the Caroubier Racetrack, ever since we had been given tickets to the races I had an aim in life, to await the great day with my friend so as to go to the races with her, where never in my life would I have dreamed of wanting to go, but now there was this absolutely absurd luck a genuine piece of luck therefore, these tickets that I spent my time being terrified of losing, for out of fear my friend might lose them, I feared everything about her, I had shouldered the entire risk, took it on my conscience, but from one day to the next the horses came closer and I didn't lose the tickets, nonetheless aware that I am one of those people who count on too big a wish, I verified and feared for the existence of the tickets several times a day. That sufficed to fill my imagination with horror scenarios and I never gave the racetrack a thought, the important thing for me being not the horses but getting there without mishap.

It is Saturday afternoon. No school. Heartstrings taut with emotion we have just said see you tomorrow. Only a few hours to wait. The phone rings. An attack is expected from the West, it is the North that flares up. I won't go into the story. Besides she barely spoke to me. Punished. Under arrest for having lost her fountain pen. Punished. I revolt. Already on the scaffold I dispute it. I am as good as dead. I pick myself up. Confront the obstacle again. Impotent before a pen. The sanction must be lifted. I make a dash for the phone. I hear a well-dressed voice hair scraped back, no makeup ever, no grammatical errors smooth-textured nylon stockings a horrible horrible politeness, I am speaking to France I gulped it is the first time and never shall I forget that I am telephoning to France herself and I recognize her voice that I am hearing for the first time. Madame I say and I tense all the muscles of my breast my hips my thighs. No she says she is being punished, oh! how Catholic of her. I circle back. I take the obstacle again. It is I, I cry who am punished. My life is ruled by unjust fortune. Have I not worked all year without a single detention. I have not lost my pen. My mother works all day long. Punish her on Monday but not on Sunday for tomorrow it is my legs that will be cut off, not hers. I am the only one who is sobbing I beg you to relent, grant me one day with my fiancée I admit my crimes I'll admit whatever you like, the pen I know it, I lost it myself, don't punish me tomorrow, not racecourse Sunday, some other time I howl down the telephone until Madame hangs up.

Now I am impatiently waiting for us to go to the semiannual concert of the French Youth Orchestra together, to which I go only in order to go with her but this I can't admit thus I am making my musical debut I am going to listen to—Bach, let's pretend, listen to Bach, another fiction, forget about Bach, Bach outshone, Bach totally and forever eliminated by the real object of my desire, the Brandenburg Concerti a fiction to accompany a duo with a marionette, an awareness of the stratagem exalts my musical debut but that is not something one can say for my friend likes to go to the French Youth Orchestra with or without me. Without her I don't go without me she will go for her I am nothing but a Brandenburg accompaniment, but she only goes, which she cannot admit, from a desire to make her puppet debut in a vast theater, immense room, big as a world with velvet armchairs which think only of her, her charm, her elegance, her embroidered socks her tartan skirt her green pullover—and to top it all off her kid gloves a classy outfit well-worth applause in the concert hall of the world. Nothing could prevent her making her gracious appearance in the dome of the Universe. In the days leading up to the day of the French Youth Orchestra the young French marionettes are flush with emotion like the cheeks of Onegin's girls. Hourly they rainbow, it's heavenly. My star is rising, I too melt with an exaltation as lofty as it is degraded. I haven't a stitch to wear. Still today these nights I have nothing to wear. Not a night without clothing crisis. I am the result of the agony suffered on the brink of famous concerts glorious evenings for my friend for me a Jewish calvary its wretchedness commensurate with the fate from which I cannot wish to hide. Concert day threatens. Not a night goes by without an attempt at confabulous transfiguration. I would do anything in the world to convince my friend, I am capable of spending my time rooting through wardrobes, picking over shelves piled with hundreds of designer sweaters hand-painted and sun-dried, artistically understated in every shade of blue, and coming up with the one and only tunic in an amazing golden shade of yellow, of attending an international meeting with hundreds of foreigners and nothing in my head but the question of what to wear, all my powers of thought trained on the key question of the outfit, the brain turned into a closet and during the sessions my silhouette adrift in the arcana of my wardrobe's extraordinary resources, coming up with fabulous combinations, researching I am naked, the foreign thinkers are invited to a banquet, I don't join them for I wish to dress peerlessly. At last one night I don a sumptuous Japanese warrior cloak with great scarab shoulders, I wear period boots to the knees, with wide straps of fine black leather. Not everybody would have the courage to dress in such a transformational manner. I alone have the key to this finery. I'm dreaming. It keeps me from sleeping.

The day of the concert approaches, a threat of delight I would gladly forgo, but can't wishing not to have to go would be tantamount to suicide, it's a catastrophe, I must go I can't go it is a double suicide on the subject of the concert, funereal music bores me to death, I have nothing to wear except my school clothes I spend my last nights praying innumerable schemes if stealing could procure me the vital outfit, would I hesitate? But not everyone can be a thief. I am ready. I have Omi's necklace in my hands. At the gate. I make my trader's debut. I try to sell the thing. A small crowd gathers. A few passersby. The necklace is scrutinized. Gold, I say. The passing Arab youths shake their heads. Something rings false. Is it too expensive? I lower the price. The Arab customers shake their heads. They go away. They turn the necklace over and over. Skeptical looks. They give the necklace back to me. Nobody buys. I ask Omi: is this necklace gold? But *natürlich!* It is gold. And yet. And yet. So I go to the concert in whatever I can put my hands on. Omi's gloves. My mother's terrific little red suede cloche hat from the days of her youth, the dye job isn't great but it is suede. Omi's necklace. It is gold. Everything a little bigger than it is a little smaller than it is a little truer a little less pure than it is but gold.

At the concert not so much as a glance at the Brandenburg Concerti I am lost in the hunt the gloves the doeskin gloves.

But all that is mere distraction from my most ancient grief. That was the work of my father. The blow. *The wound.* The event, my very own. The opening in action, what my father did to me, once, the only time, a one-time assault whose endless cruel ricochet the father doesn't foresee, how to regret the pain? it is infinitely faithful to me.

Get off the story at Government Square. Come with me to the Bab Azoun arcades, the year 1946. In the window you will see the adorable creature that fills me with a desire absolutely deaf to all commentary, to any calculation to reason, it is the *vital creature* suddenly I want it, I must have it, it is Her. It is as if it were something beyond me even outside my life. A doll says my father out of the question. He is the king. He sees nothing. Kill me I say. At your age says the king. What age, I say? Nine he says. He doesn't see. I am ninety. I am ninety million years old. I am already in the sacred amber of perpetuity. I see my apocalypse. It is her exactly. Beauty and the Beautiful. I see it all. I know it all. The Veil tells all. I can guess it all. A Moorish doll now! I lose my father. We cannot do otherwise. He doesn't see me. He believes I am a child He believes he is a father. All that is written in another time. It is as if I committed parricide in the Citroën. I know it. I commit it. In the car I am not the child. There has been a substitution. There is necessity. Kill me, I say. My father wants to hit me. But he is at the wheel. He is between anger and amazement. Anger is his kingdom. Amazement throws him off balance. A fear begins to blow through the king's inner life. There is a madwoman in his car. It is the thing he has feared for years. We are not playing. My mother ducks out the window. It's too much for her. With a flap of her wing she quits the scene. She is right. Such a scene could never take place in her presence. It takes place in another world. I go toward a death, that I know. I belong completely to the Moorish doll. I am adulterous. I enter into passion's details I want it all and I want each part I want the delicate face veil, I want the linen and silk haik, I want the silver clasp, I want the anklets I want the hidden face I want the hidden ankles I want to be the clasp and the anklets I want the baggy harem pants, I want the hidden legs I want to be the harem pants I want Algeria. I am enraged the king is enraged. We remain unmoving apart definitively living. A rain of time descends over the characters and the archive in the stubborn posture of never-again. How shall I forgive you?

All the rest is disguise.

In Oran I was in the misty decor of the promised City, in the fragrant ribbons of boulevards melting beneath my dreamy feet the shops form pyramids that rub their golden foreheads against the mountain, the streets kneel down before me whenever I want I clamber up their humps and slowly we sway across the squares, the whole city rises and falls and slowly spins around me from the blue and white painted port to the gilded mountain. The Arab cemetery has pearly teeth, it is a smile at immortality. On the squares white-clothed tables sag under the weight of pastry cigars gazelle horns the lemon sherbets dribble down the chins of the Arab beggars among whom some vague Jews. Even the little donkeys invisible but for their tails beneath their colossal burdens take a beating for laughs. They bray for laughs as the stick comes down. In Oran.

In Oran says my mother it was *Schlarafenland*. Having eyes only for Beauty, she says, I myself never saw the blind nor the amputees that you used to stare at, while I for whom there is no other God than living looked on the bright side, some people thought that Philippe Street stinks of urine, for me it wasn't a problem, if the people on the other side of the street do their business in the stairs I am astonished but I think beauty is more beautiful than squalor, the family circle has no problems, no troubles the fruit is good, the first time I saw a cart heaped with gorgeous Barbary figs I take a dish and I start to choose, that's the day I figured it out: you use pieces of old tires as gloves to peel them, says my mother, back in Oran on the bright side talking about Algeria while me, I return to the Clos-Salembier knowing that in Oran people talking about Oran speak always of gold and silver, the air on the Place d'Armes is gold dust, even the beggars have sequins, on the walls of their Oran apartments people hang paintings of the City of Oran, they are real painted pictures of Oran something the City of Algiers never inspires, whereas in Oran one glance at the Oran painting and the sun comes out. Everywhere you see benches and people seated on the benches. Shouldn't we wonder where they come from? This is one city that doesn't turn newcomers into foreigners, says the painting. That is what the benches mean, they are how people imagine the City of Oran exactly like the painting, like a City in a painting, what do they have in common with the viciousness of Algeria, in Oran people live in a painting of Oran, palm trees on the left, Oran is founded on the columns that support the blue-green tufts so that the City will never totter says the painting, to the right on the mountain its waters having stopped flowing, people picnic on Sunday Claire my husband's sister, says my mother, makes a delicious rice and ground meat omelette that I never managed to copy, the omelette of the sacred mountain. And there on the little yellow-ocher bridge which is just at the corner of the mountain and the port in the painting, that brown spot is the soul. We know a thing or two about the donkey soul of Oran, it won't budge. Push and pull till you are blue in the face, there's no getting round the donkey. My Philippe Street house, I was thinking, has a diverse population on its five floors, Spanish so-called French German called French Catholic called French and at the bottom of the heap Mohamed squats in the dark. The house donkey.

In Oran, says my mother, the water vendors come up Philippe Street with goatskins full of drinking water on their backs. People own glass demijohns. They wrap them in wet rags. People recognize themselves on the canvas. Everyone knows everyone. Only the street numbers differ. Under the stairwell is where Mohamed lives. I don't remember Mohamed says my mother. He was the envoy I say. The Muslim wandering Jew, I say. Mohamed, I was thinking, belongs to me. He came for me. To call himself Mohamed. Took his place at the base of the stairwell which had been waiting for him. Who is Mohamed? He who is—under the floors. Silence. His cardboard encampment. Now I thought when Mohamed sets up his kanoon, Oran is in order. The sentence has located its subject. During the day he does his job, right until the silent sunset which he is. On his back a coat of shadows and a handsewn patchwork of burlap bags, you wrap yourself in leftover packaging like rolls of clouds. Now and again during the week the door on the fourth-floor landing opens. It is grandma from Casablanca. My grandmother bellows down the stairwell. Mohamed! calls fourth-floor grandma. Where are you? Here I am! responds Mohamed from the black pit. Come and get something to eat, calls grandma. Rise and walk up here with your tin. And Mohamed climbs up with his empty tin can, without a murmur. Grandma fills the tin right to the brim. She looks after hers. Her who, her what, her host, her guest, her other, he has come, she doesn't know who has come, she fills the tin can. Had there not been this couple of Grandma and Mohamed the house would be like an empty tin, no doubt about that, but no one gives it a thought. The essential remains imperceptible. It is a blessing—having Mohamed in the stairwell gives the house its stubbornness. The world is complete. The wandering Mohamed is come. He bears the burden of the century on his threadbare back. Everything preexists, says my brother. Mohamed is absolute. No ancestors no descendants. A pure manifestation. The pure prophet of God and nobody.

It seems that the country's spirits as well as its anonymous prophets all squat in the Oran streets or in some cases perch in the plane trees, while they wait. "The pigeons," for instance, another Oran missive.

One day, says my mother in her letter from Oran, a patient brings my husband two pigeons. I took them to the market to have them ritually killed by the rabbi, because you don't kill animals yourself. The Street of the Jews market which later on was called Revolution Street the market of the Revolution of the Jews, that's where it was. There's a Jewish grocer, outside, sitting on the sidewalk is the rabbi with the right to kill, an old man with a bushy beard. I gave him the pigeons says my mother the Oran German that rabbi has a long and very sharp barber's razor in his teeth. He stuck one pigeon between his knees, plucked a few feathers around the neck in order to cut its throat with his razor says my mother who follows the story right to the last bit of fluff, just as he was about to cut its throat the second pigeon flew off. Whereupon he said:

—Sorry but the second pigeon has to go too.

Which is to say the first from which he had just plucked a few feathers. I say: what do you mean? says my mother. He says: you can't separate pigeons. They are couples that live and die together. There is only one pigeon, he says, says my mother, the second one. Both or none he says. Back I went with no pigeon says my mother. I said: the pigeon flew away. The second that is also the first. I didn't feel any regret says my mother, never having eaten pigeon. That's the way it is in Oran. The sacred and the holy says the old fellow you can't separate them, that's how it is in Oran, says my mother. The rabbi kills the second, the rabbi does not kill the first. A pigeon can fly away. Shouldn't we try to see where it comes from? Does the rabbi do it on purpose?

—On purpose? I ask. Of course not, says my mother, it got away from him says my mother, that means that anything can happen right to the last life or death. You know I didn't pay, says my mother. Had he killed it, he would have been paid. Not in death or in life, says my mother. In Oran, says my mother, the street is a real place. Only things happen which baffle my Germanic sense of logic.

In the family we say: the proof that the human condition is structurally flawed and genetically mortal is that my father himself made the mistake of trading paradise for Hell all the while believing he was doing the contrary.

In Algiers I fell into FrenchAlgeria, and that was the Lycée, my high school, against which I was powerless. I was already cut off from my brother, our inner life cut into two outer lives, and cut off from myself. I got lost, running in the long corridors of the Contretemps, or rather choking gut, my father gone the era had come to an end I was left to the Lycée that madness, I did my best at the intersections, I wandered around neighborhoods teeming with people, ahead of me everything shrinks the world is a puppet theater whose entryways I slip through minuscule with great difficulty, and there is no time.

I suffer from anachrony, a banal, familiar and scary mental illness: the patient is not sick, he suffers the mental anachrony of his entourage, he is surrounded by puppets, it's clear, he alone sees how everything is inside-out, upside-down, and supposedly rightway up. There is a general mental and semantic slippage. The mad take themselves for sane. Untruth is in command. Everyone believes what is not. Everyone notsees what is. The program is nonstop. My mother says people say in the countryside that the farm workers make do with very little an olive and a piece of bread, that's what they say they say they believe, they say it's believed and believe it, the country is great, but the Europeans which means the Spanish here get red wine on top of the olive and the piece of bread. In their shanties the people are content, they've got plenty to eat, the husband has work, in the shanty-towns they can heat up water, people parade around with billboards advertising the Circus. Everybody's in favor. Says my mother.

They don't mind not getting an education that's why there aren't any in my school. It's unbelievable, if my mother believes that I'll die. That's why I don't ask what she believes. Cut again.

Every five minutes Hell starts up in the Clos-Salembier all you have to do is jump aboard, and you get a good view. I jump I see all. Seeingall all by myself except for my brother is terrifying. People have aids to keep them from hearing. Every brain has the disease of translation. In a twinkling everybody says the opposite and hears the contrary. As if the same post-partum craziness had broken out in every house. The least affected say "that's the way it is." Everyone talks in wormwords and you can't change the world. There are children who go out of doors five minutes later they are in rags. That's one way of looking at things. Says my grandmother. A horrible hate lights up my brain. Out walking with my brother we make up recipes for punitive evasions. I regretted suicide was not my religion. At the end of the day I decided to get out of FrenchAlgeria for lack of Algeria, I made this decision I tucked it away, I took it out, I pondered it. My only fear was that the tip would grow dull before I was ready to leave. If I get used to it I will kill myself I threatened. I kept myself sharp.

The oldest of my oldest Algerian memories about the Plan to annihilate the Algerian being is a tale of a girl who gets cut in two.

It is in Oran on the Place d'Armes, on one of those sorts of Ferris wheel rides.

I am seven, I've been Jewish for a few years they tell me. The wheel turns, the little carriages swing back and forth. In front of me a man leans over and hugs a girl in a veil. Suddenly like a lunatic on fire she jumps like a girl who has caught fire she jumps. She is all you can see. FrenchAlgeria leaves the stage. The veil gets caught in the slats of the ride. The girl is yanked after her veil her body is trapped like a piece of meat in a grinder, she can't extract it. Her scream rings out right to the port, right to the tip of the cathedral, if a scream could halt fate, everything would stop dead. But the wheel must turn, two more times it rolls over the screaming body, a scream never before heard in the City of Oran. Everything stops now. The girl has finished screaming. Her body cut in two through its middle wrapped in the veil falls like a stone to the ground of the square to the re-lief of the spectators. A dreadful feeling of release runs through me. My ex-istence has been cut in two. It is from having seen and looked at the tor-ture that no human being should have to see, that no human being should turn away from, riveted as we were in the little carriages, the one com-pletely given over to death the other outside it is from having heard the most piercing human scream and what's more feminine rising from the pit of time in a single uninterrupted gush, as if I had heard life accusing death while spilling its blood to the very last drop. The fault grips me, here, in the little carriage. The fault, its terrible mystery. I did nothing. I was there. I am still there. I saw. I lived it. I am not dead. There is a fault. And it is my fault, somehow. I saw the crazed girl take fire veiled crazily attached to her veil leaping from the fire into the abyss. It is a tragedy that is also a City, a country, a history, the history of the one I am not, a veil keeps us apart and for this very reason I feel a veil alight a red mist on my head on my shoulders, terrified I fight it off but I don't deny it, nothing could make me deny it nothing could make me put it on, and for this reason even in spite of myself I am the bearer of a girl in a veil who is not me, I have within me a veiled girl cut in two the deadly veil the cut because I am a girl the victim's witness, cut off from the victim. I go home. I do not run. I feel that *that happened to me.* Since that accident something inside me is veiled to me.

I could no longer leave the lycée to which I was connected by the error then the death of my father. I thought only of escape.

Overnight I stopped working. I tried personality change. I thought no one would recognize me. A good student, always on the honor roll, I became a poor one, scandalously so. I don't remember that ten years earlier my father had ceased working from one day to the next on Vichy's orders. And ten years later from one day to the next I strip off my badge of honor roll I obey my father and doing nothing turns into a rebellion that precipitates me toward the destruction of my own existence. But during the doing-nothing I am searching. I meditate on the ruin of the Lycée in disguise, with all my strength with all my weaknesses I drill I dig I foment. How to blow up a mentality? A lie? A malady considered to be in the public interest and on visiting terms with the Governor-General of Algeria's daughter. But how to live without going mad in a City where people consider the presence of a Governor-General of Algeria normal? Everybody goes about their work. The streets are steep as cliffs, the cars hurtle down and are engulfed in the port. Shopkeepers have the very red or very white heads of the mentally deranged, they teeter on the thresholds of their shops, they wail like sirens, they shoo away the beggars that litter their sidewalks by barking like muleteers. Doctors are sexually and financially obsessed, they are thin, rapacious, bald, insomniac. At school the teachers are like vegetables, they are flaccid, drugged, sickly white, only the scrawny bird-headed ones come from mainland France, a minority who are in favor of Gambetta Dreyfus the Republic, for later on. I am prepared to recognize that there were some who were just and some who were honest. I am prepared to admit that there is a delightful Lycée in one part of the Lycée in disguise. I must also recognize that all human beings have a penchant for happiness, I do not deny the seduction of happiness, which doesn't keep anyone from being miserable.

As for me my one objective was to go to school with Françoise, hence I needed the school I detested. I couldn't keep myself from setting off for school too early, from getting to the K stop too early, from running to Françoise's forever-closed house too soon. Every day of my own free will I went from our prison to the insane asylum perforce disguised but not enforced. What Françoise and I liked most were the Lycée's underground passages. People say there are tunnels and we are constantly on the lookout for the door in. But before we ferret them out ding-dong goes the Lycée bell. Back we go.

I too am initiated into the art of camouflage, disguises, make-believe, pretense, masks. A kind of fibbing but only to myself forms within me as a reaction to the school's own lies. I can't keep myself from getting involved in a cavernous terrorist plot, I descend into my disquieting depths. I take myself as sole accomplice in the battle against the terrifying totalitarian Lycée plots. I dreamed up the wildest of excavation plans. I am going to catch the plan to annihilate the real Algerian being in its own trap. This is where phantomization comes in. I have become my own ghost, which brings me to the asylum management's error: having shown me how the system works. The best way to be impregnable I thought is to hide behind appearances. Whereupon I took my father's camera, broken beyond repair, which my mother had thrown in the trash but which I fished out even though beyond repair. And I made it into a tool for fabricating ghosts. I forced it on the classroom. With the vacant camera I snapped pictures of the teachers. Dozens of snapshots. Dozens of nonexistent snapshots. So I inexisted them. All. One after another. I gazed at them from the point of view of the absence of a gaze. I framed. I pressed. They posed. I clicked. I did that often. I admit they were docile and unsuspecting. They were subjects who didn't have the strength to do harm, nor good either therefore. They wobbled on their chairs and floated without sinking by flapping their plump little arms.

Never in the powder-puff Lycée did anyone mention the Algerian being. The word Algeria never sets foot here. Here in the Lycée, it is France, that is it was one great raving lie, which had taken over the whole place of the truth, thus becoming the truth.

All I wanted to say at school was: "It is not true." But this was impossible, this was an absurdity. When the nottrue extends to infinity, it is true.

My photographic scheme to destroy the make-believe did not succeed, but it didn't fail: my own classmates stopped me. A hunt. They wouldn't stop begging to look at the photos. I guessed that they didn't want to see the photos. They wanted to unmask me. Proof of their extraordinary two-facedness: they had seen through the scheme, as if they too could have imagined it, as students—initiated as they were into lying and pretense. But they were on the side of the masters. By a stroke of luck I was stopped in time: my activity lacked a philosophical basis, I thought without thinking ahead, the immateriality of my scheme was on the point of disintegrating, I prefer having been arrested, I could not have dreamed up a better end.

That was when three Muslims made their appearance at school, into the bargain in my class, it was to me that it happened, just when my wits were sharp in the fullness of my solitude, no more reveries, a blonde a brunette a redhead, Zohra Samia and Leila. They were unforgettable from day one they were future and necessary, but my life alone was aware of it, I didn't have a language, I propped up my existence with lies-and-truth words, a lie is truth, it seemed to me that there was a catwalk across the abyss, I climb up I plant myself smack in the middle, and nobody in the world could have budged me an inch. Once a mule, always a mule. For years I had despaired of ever getting close to Algeria, I gave it up, I put a world-class absurdity in its place, I abdicated even, I vanished into thin air and suddenly, out of the blue, they turn up, three of them. There is no name for what is happening to me. A kind of salvation by means of no god. Nothing special has occurred, except that now I have flesh on my soul. We were laughing. I was with them. I was attached to their presences.

I was attached to their three presences. I was with them and they were not with me, I was with them kept at arm's length by all my ghosts and all the prickly words that made us use pieces of tires as gloves, I was with them without them me who except for them could not be me. I looked all my Algerias in the face. I saw in bright glimmers how I will never gleam for them. They were headed for their lives, their turn is coming I guessed, without which I would not be me and which shines far from me, I guessed.

There was a glimmer of history. Nothing special was happening at that moment, but something was going to and I began to live for what was going to happen. My prophetic soul. The future, at long last, there was one. I made use of it as a present, I delocalized past nothings, I was no longer impatiently awaiting the Sunday trips to the racetrack, I never knocked at their door, in fact I never knew where they lived and I don't care, I needed them, from behind the bars, I called out to them silently and hopelessly.

They were my proof, I think today, did I think then, it seems to me that I did, they instantly became all others for me, all the being to come, I immediately felt therefore knew I'd had my answer. Besides they were well and truly there. The teacher called the roll and we answered cixous drif khaled lakdari present, everybody is my witness.

Inside and outside change without cease. As soon as there is some future outside enters inside exits there is alliance and return, who is inside who is out, we shall see, we don't see yet, in class I became aware of the shifts, who comes in goes out who goes out will come back in, I was with them but they were not with me, they were off in the distance no one is closer to me no one more removed. It's like a book. Before you write it it is already there, you can't talk about it, it is not there, its whole being is a little ways away very close, a few days and a few months away at the same time absolutely not before it comes into being. It may announce itself with a few pages, there's one, I tell myself, and I am distraught, given to dizzy spells, as if the spirit of the book had engulfed itself like a vortex in my breast, is it the book? it is in any case its extravagant breath. To say there's a book, I feel a book invading me, I am in the clutch of a book, is madness. You mustn't say it. Which doesn't keep you from feeling it.

In class with them, them without me, me with them in my inner life, me parked with the French, me chafing at the bars, I was in the grips of a madness I kept to myself. We would play. It seems to me. I believe. We whispered. They used to jump very high. We read Madame de Sévigné. A way of running faster than effort, lighter than speed. Under the checked pinafores. I gaze into the distance to see where they are going that I am not.

There's the book I thought if not then then not long afterward, immediately after having left Algeria I would think of that book, theirs, telling myself: I have seen the book I will not write. A stroke of fate had it begin in my class, in the next seat. There is the book I'll never write.

This time it is Algeria who speaks in front of me, I am in an old classroom, memory has cast its net over the people sitting wilted, yellowing at their desks, I remember the days to come right here where the chained century is finally over.

You've put it off long enough, I was thinking. Let's go. Move on. The hour's passed. Suddenly I wake with a start. The visit has ended.—What are you doing here? She exclaims.—You invited me I say.—No way! says She with a toss of her curly head. I see that Zohra Drif, at Her side has no idea what all this is about. I launch into a long diatribe. I shall complain. I had trouble freeing myself to come. I had no desire to. I came because she invited me. Ten years you said. Ten days I mean. I feel a violent irritation. What am I doing here? Who's keeping me here? I myself am keeping myself here? When I could get up and go? All I ever did was dream of leaving and I am about to launch into a speech? I brought myself up short.—My mistake I say, I shall make amends this very day, I am taking the first train for France, I say. When does it leave? Tonight. Afraid of missing it I leave on the spot. The station was at the other end of town of course. You have to cross the City from top to bottom. A single interminable hill that goes down and doesn't come back up. The main thing is be on your way. When I arrive in France, I shall write a letter to Zohra Drif I thought

Another solitary reverie I thought.

—Wait! says my separated brother, him still outside me in the process of leaving this outside that I no longer want to hear about, which for years we called Algeria although that wasn't its real name. Wait a minute! says my childhood and everything within me that is my brother. Don't go now! Just when Kader, or maybe Idir, is coming doyouremember that Kabyle boy who is a little in love with you, Idir? I say, I have no memory of Kader or Idir. It's my brother who brings him back to me. He was in love? It's my brother who has a photo of Kader who might be Idir. Did I love him? Kader's photo smiles at me with fierce shyness. Or maybe it's my brother who knew he had a crush and I didn't notice. Or maybe it's the violence of the anachrony that was our undoing. The times only separunited with stroke after distancing stroke. And yet in another later on, it seems to me I remember I might have loved him. It seems to me now that he is coming back. He is thin, full of formality. Does he give me his hand? While we stand there without moving, as if already congealed in the resin of a photograph. Do I feel the dry palm of his hand, or is that an encounter the story wants to slip into my memory? or graft onto me? I daren't assert that I don't remember Kader or rather Idir. Do I envision Idir shy to match my shyness? It seems to me—yes? And we doyouremember his great gentleness, a blonde light as a gazelle ready to flee toward us, Idir or Kader says my brother it's Idir I say but maybe Kader, who sways gently between two names, at the end of the Clos-Salembier drive, facing me from the other end of the drive, I look at him, my face turned toward his, we are strange, a strange absence of violence makes a halo around us, thick hair, narrow-chested, ready to flee toward one another, don't move! says the author of everything-that-happens-as-if-it-didn't, we don't move, now there's the photo, we see: *the meeting whose other name is adieu.* All that could happen and will not happen on this earth that is what leaves luminous traces in the Drive, we look at one another once and for all the times which will never be and we think simultaneously that it is too soon in our surroundings for That. Silently from lip to lip a yes flutters between Idir Kader my brother and me. Everything that is still unsayable is already readable. Brief wedding dream. The photo remains. We see the palm trees, the banana trees, the gate. To the right Fips the dog fades out.

The second pigeon is gone. The old man who kills turns up his empty hands. I flew away in a single stroke, neck plucked, not knowing whether I was following the other one in life or in death. There where death is already at work I thought, life begins. I arrived in France, bare-necked, it was so cold everywhere, inside, outside, up down and all along, I searched for myself everywhere and in vain. No I hadn't come to France, that winter, I hadn't in fact ever really thought about the winter called France, I had only at long last left Algeria plucked of the feathers that protect the place of life.

After-the-departure, according to my mother, nothing changed, everything was fine except that she no longer went to the Mozabite's to buy meat but to the Galeries. What wasn't fine was that she had committed suicide without meaning to, first by introducing the fateful figure of hunchback Maria into her own house, then because of the elevator business she herself had initiated.

— Out of pity I got myself thrown in prison says my mother in a calm voice. When the French left Algeria I inherited a little hunchback her employer had let go. I kept *Maria* says my mother, whose real name I never knew, a cleaning woman for whom I did a great deal of good. All the French had left. The concierge's lodging is vacant and I am the one who tells poor *Maria* she may live there. She moves in with her brother-in-law her sister their children. Her brother-in-law the concierge promptly goes into business selling bras and panties to pregnant women in the building's entry hall where the patients can now barely squeeze by. The concierge says my mother in a well-modulated voice was a crook. Next there was the business with the elevator. There was an elevator that worked with coins. This money serves to pay the repairman a very handy Frenchman who is still around. Once I left to go and visit my daughter in Paris my mother tells me. I gave the money-box key to *Maria,* when I am not there take the change and pay the repairman, I say says my mother. But helping this woman was not a great success. I didn't find any money in the box says *Maria* and the elevator was not working when I returned says my mother. But there were two tenants in the building who saw it all. Two young men with a very good pastry shop on the ground floor, says my mother. I told *Maria:* Listen *Maria* which is to say maybe Farida the money is not in the box, but of course she's not listening to me. I say: if we can't use the elevator we will no longer be able to work here, the women in labor won't be able to come up. The Clinic cannot function. It is unacceptable for you to help yourself to the money. As far as I am concerned such a thing is out of the question. If it continues I'll have to have a word with the police. Right away she took the initiative beginning with the two young men she denounced them to the police as homos, she had them expelled, they have to leave on the double, without their pastry shop. Next it was the neighbor on the seventh floor who didn't have his furniture any more. The neighbor saw his furniture down below. The concierge in the hallway selling bras for pregnant women was now sitting in the neighbor's chair. The neighbor didn't say boo, for fear *Maria* took the initiative. That Farida whom we'd tried calling Maria and who had become the angel of hate with her silver teeth. She would cackle. Sneering with her silver roots and taste for vengeance.

Next *Maria* took the initiative with me. I had delivered her, everything went smoothly, she had the concierge's baby, I delivered her sister also the wife of the concierge. Right after that I don't know what gets into the belly of her twisted mind. The police turn up at the Clinic.—Someone's got something against you the police announce. And they hustle me off to the judge. Can you imagine! There are newborns in the trash cans! I spent a night in jail and toward the evening of the following day I arrive in *Barberousse.* The same only different I thought, Barberousse Prison tops the City of Algiers on the brow of the City of Oran, *Santacrousse* Chapel. Barbarossa, says my mother, everybody's heard of it, nobody knows it. It is an experience I was happy there. When I recovered from my fright and my first night in jail on a slab of cement, I slept like a log on a straw pallet, I was happy in prison. There were about ten women in detention. Each of us told the story of our life. I felt relieved, says my mother, because I wasn't responsible for the Clinic, thanks to prison I am off the hook, I can't be upset with myself, it is the first time in years that I can relax, and furthermore says my mother, I can joke with the others. The youngest drummed on the plastic buckets all night long singing and dancing. There is an entire brothel, that is the madam, two jewels of girls, a little cousin, who every day receive a big hamper of food. We shared everything. The one I feel sorry for is Fatma I mean Barta one of my veiled cleaning women who brings a hamper to me in prison every day: it was uphill every inch of the way. I wrote my one regret which was that after having found my notebook one day, it disappeared again. Don't go losing what I am telling you. It's all that remains to me of Algeria. Meanwhile my son tells *Maria:* and in addition you want your month's wages? So what does she do? Right there on the spot she takes the initiative. She goes off to the police station, she says: they want to blackmail me. In a twinkling my son finds himself in prison. But on the men's side, among whom quite a collection of fairies. All the same *Maria* and the concierge were poor souls. Taking pity on them wasn't a great success for me. Might she have thought she could move into my apartment furnished by the seventh-floor neighbor?

She was a nasty one the angel of hate so nasty so crafty that when the time for the trial came when the judge asked her: where are your witnesses, she had only herself and her brother-in-law as witnesses so the judge says: you are the sole witness? So perhaps you are an accomplice? In a flash she understood, and right away she says: there is no witness me I didn't see a thing. Everybody goes free but imprisoned forever in terror and evil. That bunch of poor-souls-all-the-same, they wanted me out of there. For their sake I wasn't leaving. I wasn't going to leave now and turn the place over to them. Common sense was what they lacked. That lot plagued me and I plagued them. I was scared of them and they were scared of me. They wanted me gone and I was still around, they were with me in the building without me being with them. The nice one was the prison director who later brought me his wife and daughters to deliver. They used to walk past the concierge and his bra display to take the elevator which worked when I was there. The Clinic, says my mother, I really liked it, everyone was always very nice and it was a going concern, in the morning we are always up by seven and later I went to the market which I preferred doing by myself with a big *empty* basket filled to overflowing coming back I took a little porter who carried my basket, after that I told them what to do in the kitchen, you have to post the menus at noon I always cooked the steaks, after there are rounds, the visits and the deliveries often at night. The main thing was the deliveries of course. When the baby's on the way the Staff comes it's a big party, the cook forgets about the cooking, the cleaning lady forgets about the cleaning. The Staff laughs and shouts that way the woman giving birth doesn't have time not to be brave, and now here's the baby. And I always see to it that there's not a drop of blood on the floor. A pair of scissors and forceps for the cord, next to nothing. I really loved all that. One thing is frightening, that's the *placenta previa,* in the final months when it gets below the head you have an obstruction, the placenta *blocking the head like a door.* The woman loses a lot of blood. But fortunately I knew what to do: you must break the waters. And as soon as you have broken them, bang, the head comes down, that produces a hemostasis, that's it, no more blood, the infant saves his mother and himself. It is a very simple gesture, remember: break the waters. But in the end for nothing in the world would they have wished to miss out on prison. Prison was the unforeseen gift, the apotheosis of Algeria, the very taste and smell of the unforgettable. In other words bliss.

Still those last years were spoiled. Right up to the day I didn't jump at the opportunity, *Maria's* fault again. And like an idiot I killed myself. I could have sold the Clinic to an Algerian midwife but I didn't do it for lack of common sense, all because of *Maria* I didn't jump at the opportunity to sell the Clinic when the time was ripe. As a result one morning, I go to declare a birth at city hall. And when I come back, no more Clinic. The police have sealed it off, the staff's lab coats removed, the patients sent away.—What are you doing here? I say.—Ah! you're not the only one say the police. I went downstairs. The neighbor from the seventh floor says: You're not going to let them get away with it? I say: Scissors against stone, I've had enough. I'm leaving. I take the nameplate down, and the Clinic ceases to exist.

I took what I needed in the only suitcase I owned, the Mess, the one that was already a mess when it came from Osnabrück, a nightie, a few snapshots, and the next day I had nothing but my stories. And the Mess in the basement.

There are so many mistakes and so little common sense. I wasn't up to it. I myself let that nemesis called "Maria" into my house, I opened the door even before she knocked. Overnight the Clinic went down lock, stock, and barrel.

In 1955 I left slamming the door, vowing never to return. Afterward I returned each year but from in back or on the side, I didn't look for the door, I went to the Clinic to visit my mother and my root.

In 1971 one morning I say: I am going to the Clos-Salembier where I have not been since 1955, don't go says my brother, I went all the same I don't know why, as if I went in a dream, I did the opposite to what I wanted to do, I had said I wouldn't go, and I went, I left the Clinic, I went to the General Post Office where I took the K without waking up. In front of the house there was no house, I had expected as much but seeing what you expect is another surprise. I was standing before a high white wall. There was no door, and instead of leaving on the spot, I began to look for the door, I could not do otherwise. On the other side of the square wall on the third side I found a little iron gate. I'm leaving I thought and knocked at what was not a door but a closing. I knocked. No answer. I'm leaving I say and the closing opens a sliver. I should have apologized instead of which I find myself gesticulating I would like to come in I say, I point, toward nothing but a white wall which rises in its turn from behind the gate. And the gate closes in my face. And here I am running away as if to get across a vacant lot with barbed wire that was not there, I catch the K on the run, wondering what I am doing there and here what am I doing, running away, toward the past or the future without knowing why and because I couldn't do otherwise. Something's blocked in my head I thought. You must break the bag of waters, says my mother, otherwise that's the end of the infant inside the mother as well as the mother. I must have wept.

But now the more I talk about it and the more I go back there especially with my brother the more I feel at home in the Clos-Salembier now and retrospectively, to the degree I was thrown out assailed expulsed nailed to the gate so I am at home there now I am no longer chained up and now I talk about it especially with Idir Kader and my brother, the Clos-Salembier has become part of me and I am attached to each of the places I fled and each hated hateful moment is for me a vital transfigure that I wouldn't exchange for any kinder gentler moment in the world.

I've never wanted to write about Algeria this unknown native land whose high closed blankness I skirted for so many years, the idea of writing never even crossed my mind nonetheless it would be the most unexpected thing that has ever happened to me if all of a sudden a book swooped down and picked me up bodily and carried me off to the Clos-Salembier in spite of my hesitations after all these years, I thought all that already in 1994 and I've also noticed of late that shortly before dawn before sunrise opening the window to hear, that is to imagine I heard, in the most distant distance, the barking of a dog but so far off you might call it I told myself a reflection of barking like the memory of a dream of barking or who knows like the slight barking of the memory of a dog, a sad old reverie and then in the morning I began to listen to, then to fear not hearing, then to hope for, and almost always to hear as if it were coming not across space but across the space of time, the increasingly familiar barking, right up to the day when, as if I woke suddenly after forty years of sleep, I believed I recognized and right away I really did recognize the sound of Fips's voice. This is the way the voice of a long dead son resonates, loud and clear, with undeniable truth, but so far away, and brief. The memory of a voice. The resonant trace of Fips's voice forty years after his death. I could no longer put off the book which didn't stop calling me whenever I opened the window of darkness. I sat up in my bed in the middle of the night and with the soft lead of the pencil always within reach I scrawled in the dark: *The whole time I was living in Algeria I would dream of one day arriving in Algeria.*

About the Author

Hélène Cixous is a French writer, philosopher, playwright, critic, and activist who continues to influence writers, scholars, and feminists around the world. Her recent works include *The Day I Wasn't There* and *The Third Body,* both published by Northwestern University Press, and *Veils* (with Jacques Derrida), *Portrait of Jacques Derrida as a Young Jewish Saint, The Writing Notebooks,* and *Dream I Tell You.*

Avant-Garde & Modernism Collection

General Editor
Rainer Rumold

Avant-Garde & Modernism Studies

General Editors
Marjorie Perloff
Rainer Rumold